VALUES
AT THE
CORE

**How Human Values Contribute
to the Rise of Nations**

VALUES
AT THE
CORE

**How Human Values Contribute
to the Rise of Nations**

Thomas Grandjean
ChinHwee Tan

 World Scientific

NEW JERSEY · LONDON · SINGAPORE · BEIJING · SHANGHAI · HONG KONG · TAIPEI · CHENNAI · TOKYO

Published by

World Scientific Publishing Co. Pte. Ltd.

5 Toh Tuck Link, Singapore 596224

USA office: 27 Warren Street, Suite 401-402, Hackensack, NJ 07601

UK office: 57 Shelton Street, Covent Garden, London WC2H 9HE

Library of Congress Cataloging-in-Publication Data
Names: Grandjean, Thomas, author. | Tan, ChinHwee, author.
Title: Values at the core : how human values contribute to the rise of nations /
    Thomas Grandjean, ChinHwee Tan, Trafigura Pte Ltd, Singapore.
Description: Hackensack : World Scientific, 2020. | Includes bibliographical references.
Identifiers: LCCN 2020045096 | ISBN 9789811228520 (hardcover) |
    ISBN 9789811230387 (paperback) | ISBN 9789811228537 (ebook) |
    ISBN 9789811228544 (ebook other)
Subjects: LCSH: Economic development. | Economic policy. | Social policy. |
    Equality. | Values--Social aspects.
Classification: LCC HD82 .G636 2020 | DDC 170--dc23
LC record available at https://lccn.loc.gov/2020045096

British Library Cataloguing-in-Publication Data
A catalogue record for this book is available from the British Library.

For any available supplementary material, please visit
https://www.worldscientific.com/worldscibooks/10.1142/12048#t=suppl

Desk Editor: Lai Ann

Typeset by Stallion Press
Email: enquiries@stallionpress.com

Printed in Singapore

A highly readable book. Grandjean and Tan do have a compelling message. Success stories of nations are never based only on material and economic factors. Cultural identity, level of trust and motivation play a crucial role. This book provides important messages both for business and government leaders.

Esko Aho
Former Prime Minister, Finland

Using vivid examples from around the world, Grandjean and Tan show that values play a crucial role in shaping the economic success of a country — a compelling antidote to the usual litany of purely economic factors.

Lord Mervyn King
Former Governor, Bank of England
Professor of Economics, Stern School of Business,
New York University
Professor of Law, School of Law, New York University

"This readable book by Grandjean and Tan reduces the complexity of national economic performance to a simple proposition — that the values which govern how members of society relate to one another determine what the society is capable of at any particular point in time, given the overall situation and the state of technology. Values at the Core is not an abstract theory of history. It is a practical analysis of the vital indicators which measure the health and vitality of a society like the willingness to work hard and save. The book is peppered with illustrations from different parts of the world. That the proposition becomes so obvious after reading the book attests to the clarity and persuasiveness of the authors. Thus economic development is nothing more than the result of good health. It is values which make the world valuable."

George Yeo
Former Minister of Foreign Affairs, Singapore
Chairman & Executive Director, Kerry Logistics Network

This is a brave attempt to combine cultural values with economics. It is thought-provoking and some areas will resonate with the reader and some may be more challenged. Residing in Canada, I believe multiculturalism is a strength, and in the world of business, this case is supported by hundreds of academic and market studies. Multiculturalism requires more work but leads to better long-term results. The other areas explored in the book and the recommendations resonate strongly with my experiences living and working in Europe, Asia, and North America. Definitely worth a read.

Mark Machin
President, Canada Pension Plan Investment Board

The importance of values at the core of cultures and peoples has come to be appreciated more strongly this year than ever before in our lifetime. The global pandemic and the ensuing financial crisis have exposed cracks in organisations and societies with inequalities in income as well as in access to education, healthcare, digital tools, opportunities and fair treatment. These unprecedented events are also accompanied by the rapid pace of technological advances and their accelerated adoption on a global scale. The eventual outcomes of these trends will be determined by the manner in which human behaviour intersects with technological progress, through ethical frameworks and policies that are strongly influenced by values. Indeed, how values at the individual, institutional and community levels influence the actions of citizens and their countries ultimately determine the rise and fall of nations through history. This very readable book by Grandjean and Tan elucidates how values come to shape economies and humanity.

Subra Suresh
President & Distinguished University Professor, Nanyang Technological University, Singapore

Building on their extensive knowledge of cultural differences across the world, Thomas Grandjean and ChinHwee Tan make a compelling case that human values are a critical determinant of economic prosperity. While one-size-fits-all policies are bound to fail, they explain how each country needs to find its own path to unleash its potential. An invaluable analysis!

Jean-Baptiste Michau
Professor of Economics, Ecole Polytechnique, France

A fresh and original insight into how human values shape long term economic prosperity. I love how ChinHwee Tan and Thomas Grandjean incorporate fascinating examples around the world in such an elegant way. With economic power shifting increasingly towards Asia, and other non-western regions, this timely analysis provides a radically different perspective that standard economic theory too often neglected.

Amelia Xiao Fu
Chief Economist of Commodity Research, Bank of China International

The remarkable success of societies with a Confucian heritage (Japan, then South Korea, and now China), some with western-style constitutional government, some not, has reinvigorated interest in the role that values and institutions play in economic and political development. Grandjean and Tan's timely exploration and reflections warrant wide readership.

Sir Paul Tucker
Research Fellow, Harvard Kennedy School
Author of *Unelected Power*

In my many years dealing with Tan as a professional investor, his sharp analytics and observation beyond just the numbers is the foundation for this book. Tan's approach on social, cultural and political dimension as he looks through each investment due diligence case is translated into a macro-level framework succinctly in this work. A good read for those who wants to aspire to have an edge in analysis.

Khalid Al-Rumaihi
Chief Executive Officer, Bahrain Mumtalakat Holding Company

Contents

Foreword

I first met ChinHwee Tan at a dinner organized by Ambassador of Finland Paula Parviainen in her home. We chatted late into the night about the success of the Finland and Scandinavian model. We discussed how our collective values as people, cultures and countries have played a key role in the rise and fall of nations. Our Nordic model comprises both political and economic policies, leveraging on the cultural and social norms of the ecosystem. Specifically, trust forms a vital component in the ability of citizens in Nordic societies to understand one another and work together to resolve conflicts, make inclusive decisions and ultimately work towards a brighter future for all. Too often though, trust and other cultural norms are ignored when making cross-country comparisons, leading to erroneous expectations in the ability of the Nordic model to be replicated elsewhere.

This concept of linking economic destiny with cultural and political economy is not new; in fact, it was first discussed by the most famous economist of all times, Adam Smith's 1776 classic *The Wealth of Nations*. However over the years, mathematical modelling came to dominate the field of economics, with contributions from softer sciences such as behavioral psychology largely ignored until only recently with few Nobel Prizes in Economic Sciences awarded for economic theories that incorporate the actual behavior of humans.

When are these values ingrained in us? Why does it seem like they seldom change? Is it the work of nature or nurture? Context is key and there are many instances of societies with values at their 'core' that have allowed them to celebrate an environment conducive to growth, while others have remained stagnant. Indeed, together with a bit of luck, it is the potential within us that determines our economic destiny.

A highly readable book. Grandjean and Tan do have a compelling message. Success stories of nations are never based only on material and economic factors. Cultural identity, level of trust and motivation play a crucial role. This book provides important messages both for business and government leaders. It attempts to better the understanding of how economies work and the values that have come to shape them.

Esko Aho
Former Prime Minister, Finland

Preface

People around the world grow up with different sets of values guiding their vision and behavior. Too often neglected by economists, these values constitute key factors in the way economies are structured and their potential for further growth. To a large extent, they explain why Japan has gone through multiple lost decades; why Nordic countries accept the highest tax rates in the world, making their societies much more equal; why China has such a large trade surplus with the United States; or why some nations become stuck in a middle-income trap. It is these values, coupled with the right policies, that ultimately determine the economic destiny of nations. In this book, we explore how the combination of human values and policies affects national economic outcomes. We focus on key values conducive to growth: are people of a given nation, on average, hard-working, thrifty, trusting, or risk-averse? The harder people work, the higher the growth potential. The willingness and ability to save determines, to a large extent, whether a country will grow through investments and exports versus consumption. Trust goes a long way towards explaining wealth and income inequalities and the role that governments can play in minimizing these inequalities. Economies with highly risk-averse citizens will stall. We also identify policies that, in our view, have the greatest impact on economies. Market forces are essential for further growth. Political stability, in particular the absence of armed conflicts, is more conducive to growth than any specific form of government. An educated workforce breeds innovation and productivity. Corruption, on the other hand, can seriously derail an economy. Sound fiscal and monetary policies are vital for an economy to go through its cycles and prevent crises. This book bridges the gap between values and policies, recognizing that it is only by taking into consideration these two set of factors that we can truly understand how economies work.

Thomas Grandjean and ChinHwee Tan

Acknowledgments

This book is dedicated to our families and company team members around the world.

Much of this book was written during the Covid-19 pandemic. The inability to travel restricted our movements but also gave us an opportunity to get our thoughts together and ensure that we would make the most of those highly unusual times.

ChinHwee wishes to thank Michelle, Brian, Kylie, and Sarah who have kept him going. Nothing is more important than the values his parents and siblings have passed on to him, which he prays that his children will follow.

Thomas is greatly indebted to his family who has supported him throughout all those years: Yvonne, Monique, Nathalie, and Pierre. Without them this book would not have been possible.

Together, we would like to express our gratitude to the many colleagues and friends who have provided invaluable feedback to this book, in particular Manuel Aros, Philip Goetz, Rajat Maroo, Reiko Yamagishi, Taisuke Imaizumi, Xiaojun Chen, Andy Kalusivikako, Vanessa Wang, Andy Cheng, Fion Sim, Jean-Baptiste Michau, Zachary Wang, Dr Juliana Chan, and Dr KaiSyng Tan.

Finally, we are very grateful to the entire team at World Scientific, in particular Chua Hong Koon and Lai Ann, for all their support and a very efficient production process.

"We must build a prosperous society, and for this we must encourage thrift and hard work, qualities which will make for a high rate of capital investment and growth in industry and in agriculture. In this process, we should help as many as possible of have-nots to become haves."

Lee Kuan Yew
Speech on the Financial Policy of the Central Government
December 1964

Prologue

It had been an eventful day for Anja. In the late afternoon, she was sipping coffee with her friend Olivia in one of the many coffee shops nestled along the main avenue of Uppsala, a city located 40 miles north of Stockholm where both of them lived and worked. She would gather with Olivia on most weekends, bringing Klara along, her one-year-old daughter. Their routine typically involved buying a few accessories and finishing off the day with a drink. As she did every time the weather permitted, Anja had left Klara outside the coffee shop for her afternoon nap. She believed, as did most of her friends with young children, that exposure to fresh air makes babies healthier by putting them in an environment where they are less likely to be exposed to germs.

As she gazed through the window from time to time to ensure that all was fine with Klara, a middle-aged woman caught her attention. The woman was standing next to the pram, looking around and seeming very puzzled. She then suddenly took hold of Klara, lifting her from the pram. Horrified, Anja jumped out of her seat and rushed outside to confront the woman.

"What do you think you're doing?" Anja asked in Swedish, taking hold of her daughter.

"I'm sorry, I do not speak your language," stammered the woman, visibly shaken.

"What are you doing?" Anja repeated, this time in English.

"Well I thought this baby had been abandoned."

"She certainly has not. I'm her mother."

"But then why would you leave her on the streets?"

"Because that's what we do in this country. For them to get some fresh air."

"What if someone stole your baby?"

"Why would anyone do that?"

Still very confused but also embarrassed by this turn of events, the woman apologized to Anja for what had happened. She had been trying to help, wrongly believing that the child was in danger. A short discussion followed, during which Anja learnt that the woman was from the United States touring the Nordic countries on holiday with her husband, who stood a few yards away, not keen to get involved but seemingly quite amused by the situation his wife had landed herself into.

Now back at home preparing dinner together with her husband, Anja gave the incident some more thought. It had never occurred to her that someone would try to steal her baby. In a city of close to 200,000 inhabitants, there were many people she did not know, but even then, she felt safe in the knowledge that they would never cause harm to her or her daughter. Tourists were a common sight, drawn to local landmarks such as the cathedral, medieval castles, and gardens, but they had never caused any issues.

Then again, when she travelled to other countries, she had to admit to herself that she was more careful with her belongings and, at least outside Nordic countries, she would not leave her daughter alone outside on the streets. Even in Uppsala, although she had not realized it at first, Anja had become more cautious. She felt that the city had changed in the past decade. It had welcomed a large number of foreigners, which had made her more wary when going out in the evening. Perhaps she was becoming a bit paranoid, telling herself stories. After all, she had never experienced any problem herself. It was probably a natural reaction to something Anja was unfamiliar with. Time would tell whether those fears would prove justified or not.

*

Mrs. Chen was again shouting from the other side of the shop, complaining about some items on a shelf which had run out and not been restocked.[1] "Let the old woman shout," thought Karabo. She had somehow gotten used to the Chinese storekeeper's frequent bouts of anger. One of the customers who had just walked in stared at Karabo, wondering what was going on. Karabo rolled her eyes, eliciting a smile from the customer.

Karabo had been working as a shop assistant in central Gaborone, Botswana's capital city, for the past eight months. She knew the city well, having been born and raised there. Her father worked as a security guard whilst her mother was employed as an administrative assistant in a state-owned company. Karabo never had much interest in studying. She dropped out of secondary school and was glad to be done with it. Now in her early twenties, she aspired to enjoy the best years of her life, spending most of her time with friends and family. She had always been a joyous and carefree person, rarely anxious about anything. Olebogeng, the man she had been dating for the past two years, was a wonderful companion. He was employed as a bank clerk just a few blocks away from Mrs. Chen's shop. They would get together during most lunch times, where their friends and colleagues would often join, and communicated throughout the day through text messages. They planned to get married soon, possibly next year.

One aspect about her life that Karabo disliked was working for that dreadful shop owner. She wondered how she had managed to keep up with Mrs. Chen for eight months; it had felt like an eternity. Mrs. Chen would constantly accuse her assistant of not trying hard enough, criticizing her for her perceived lack of dedication, punctuality, and organization. Mrs. Chen was a control freak, expecting total servitude and long hours of work. Once she even told Karabo that she should be grateful for the opportunity to work at the shop. It was not as if the pay was any good, barely above the minimum wage. Karabo felt exploited; how could she survive with such a meager salary? Whenever she did her grocery shopping or went out with friends for drinks or a meal, prices everywhere seemed to be on the rise. At some point, her income would no longer cover her expenses.

Even after eight months into the job, Karabo realized that she knew almost nothing about Mrs. Chen (not that she wanted to know more). The shop owner never spoke about her personal life, but anyway she did not seem to have any, devoting all her time to the shop, so there was probably not much to confide about. Karabo did not even know what her first name was, always calling her by her surname. She would see her meet up with a few other Chinese women, but only once or twice a week. Mrs. Chen seemed to have no family and few friends. Occasionally she would switch on the television set at the back of the shop and watch some Chinese show. Karabo wondered why anyone would come all the way from China and work tirelessly all day long for so little benefit. It was not like Mrs. Chen was making millions, or if she was, she was hiding them very well. Mrs. Chen never let Karabo handle the finances of the shop either. The bookkeeping was entirely managed by the Chinese shop owner, who also handled all the payments from customers and locked the cash registry whenever she was away. Mrs. Chen had clearly no trust for her employee; she even had three surveillance cameras installed in the shop. She had told Karabo that this was to protect the shop against shoplifters, but Karabo knew that it was also a way to monitor her behavior in the shop.

With Christmas fast approaching, Karabo was looking forward to spending the festive season with family and friends and taking some time off. Mrs. Chen had told her that there would be more work at the shop with many more customers during that period and that she was counting on her. Karabo had considered going to work during those days, but that thought only briefly crossed her mind. Given the way that she was being treated, there was little reason to please her employer. And that's assuming Mrs. Chen could be pleased; there would be no sign of gratitude from that woman.

But today Karabo brushed all those thoughts aside. It was payday, a day she had been eagerly waiting for. She looked forward to meeting up with Olebogeng and their friends in the evening. They would end up going to the malls, checking out a few items that she had read up in magazines, maybe watch a movie. Payday was a day Karabo felt free, free from those monetary constraints that forced her back into that Chinese shop the very next day.

*

Mrs. Chen had been observing Karabo from her seat behind the cashier. As was often the case, she was far from impressed with what she saw. Then again, she had gotten used to her assistant's lack of commitment. It was not just Karabo; all the previous assistants had displayed the same careless attitude.

Mrs. Chen, now in her late fifties, had arrived in Botswana with her husband six years earlier from the Chinese province of Fujian. Back in China, her husband had started a business providing basic materials to the construction industry with his wife helping out with administrative matters. It proved a difficult life. The couple struggled to compete with larger, well-established companies. With debts mounting, they were forced into a frugal life, living in a cramped apartment and counting every cent.

One day, her husband had had enough. He suggested they migrate to Botswana, which Mrs. Chen had never heard of before. A childhood friend of her husband had moved there a decade earlier and was apparently doing well supplying spare parts for the mining industry. He described Botswana as a land full of opportunities for those willing to work hard. Her husband became convinced that they would live a better life in this faraway country. What was there to lose? There was little holding them back in China, since their parents had passed away and they had no child to look after.

After what seemed like an endless trip, they finally landed in Gaborone and were picked up at the airport by her husband's friend who drove them around the city. The place was not as run down as what Mrs. Chen had expected after watching documentaries about Africa. The buildings were quite modern, and the streets looked clean. The city felt safe. Their temporary accommodation, arranged by their guide for the day, was basic but clean and decently furnished.

Within a few weeks, her husband had opened a shop selling not only clothes and furniture, but also footwear and mobile phones. Almost every product was imported from China. Business picked up quickly as it had for most Chinese-owned shops in the city; product quality was not great, but prices were unbeatable. Competition came, not so much from locally-owned shops, but from other Chinese-owned shops, of which there were already quite a few in Gaborone. With her husband frequently travelling and involved in another local venture, Mrs. Chen was tasked with handling day-to-day operations at the shop.

Although the shop was doing well, one constant headache throughout those years had been her shop assistants. If it were down to Mrs. Chen, she would have hired a Chinese assistant, but those pesky local laws prevented this: shop assistants had to be locals. And she needed an assistant as she could not do all the work by herself. Karabo, her latest assistant, turned out to be no different from the others who preceded her: often late for work, always standing idly by, playing with her phone, and chatting with friends and customers. It seemed they had no motivation to work and no appreciation for the job they were offered. They also could not be trusted: the previous assistant had been let go for stealing from the cashier.

Karabo complained about her salary all the time. But the salary was no different from what other Chinese shops were paying. Besides, Mrs. Chen felt it should be more than enough to put some money aside since Karabo had few expenses as she lived with her parents. The problem was that her assistant was wasting her income on frivolous things such as shopping and nights out. She seemed to be out with friends almost every evening. Every few weeks she would show up at the shop dressed in clothes that Mrs. Chen had never seen before. No wonder she had little money left by the end of the month. Mrs. Chen had thought of increasing Karabo's salary towards the end of the year, but certainly not with that kind of attitude in her work.

The lack of dedication would become evident in the coming days. There were just a few weeks to go to Christmas, the busiest (and most profitable) time of the year for Mrs. Chen. She was convinced that Karabo would not show up. Not having an assistant during that busy period meant a hectic schedule and lost income. Her previous shop assistants had come up with all sorts of excuses to justify their absence. One of them had told her that their mother had passed. Mrs. Chen had sympathized with her employee's plight, until the same assistant used the same excuse the following year, not realizing her mistake. Mrs. Chen felt betrayed and became convinced that local people should never be trusted.

Introduction

Throughout the history of mankind, the rise of societies, whether civilizations, nations, or communities, has been a story of *human* achievement. From the rise of the Akkadian empire in ancient Mesopotamia to the re-emergence of modern China, people constitute the basic denominator upon which societies build their success. Great leaders play a major role in this process, providing vision and an organizational structure that leads to further development, but ultimate success depends equally on everyone else that forms part of a society.

The way people around the world think and behave is guided by a complex system of values, attitudes, and beliefs, often loosely defined as 'culture'. Given the wide range of interpretations of what culture entails and the sometimes-overlapping definitions of values, attitudes, and beliefs, in this book we refer mainly to values, defined as principles that we closely identify with and which drive us throughout our lives. For most of us, they are acquired during childhood as we collect and assimilate information from the environment that we grew up in, not only through social interaction with family members, friends, schoolmates, and teachers, but also through media, such as television, radio, newspapers, and social media. We may not realize it, but values are deeply rooted into each of us. As a result, they seldom change over time, and even when they do change, they do so very slowly. Most of us feel that we belong to a group, whether it is a nation, a community, a family, a social class, an ethnicity, a town, or a

1

religion. People share many of the same values within the group they belong to and tend to transmit those values from one generation to the next.

The ability of societies to generate wealth over a sustained period of time ultimately determines their destiny. Only wealthy societies can afford a large-scale modern military establishment, ensure the well-being of their citizens, and grow their sphere of influence. Likewise, economic mismanagement can precipitate their downfall. In the words of economists Glenn Hubbard and Tim Kane: "The existential threat to great civilizations is less barbarians at the gates than self-inflicted *economic* imbalance within."[1] Perhaps now more than ever, wealth is power.

The generation of wealth, through the use and exchange of scarce resources, is the focus of economics. Ultimately, it is a study of human behavior at the individual level or in aggregate. In its quest to become more scientific and 'objective', much of the economic profession has considered humans to be fully rational economic agents solely motivated by their self-interest, a process that can be traced back to John Stuart Mill's *Principles of Political Economy* in 1848. From the late 19th century, the use of mathematical models became increasingly widespread. This scientific rigor has allowed economists to make great progress in many aspects of economic life, deepening our understanding of the role of markets, firms, and governments. But in doing so, economists have at times forgotten that models are a simplified representation of the real world, that the assumptions underlying their models reflect a deviation from the complexity of human societies. Experiments on those assumptions, as pioneered by economist Vernon Smith in the late 1970s, revealed that people's behaviors are guided by factors that are too often absent from economic models, such as fairness, confidence, tolerance, integrity, trust, compassion, or reciprocity. Economics could never attain the scientific excellence of physics, for the simple reason that the behavior of humans will never be as consistent or predicted with the same level of accuracy as the behavior of atoms or other particles.

Different Societies, Different Economic Outcomes

Why do some communities prosper within a generation or two wherever they migrate, controlling an outsized chunk of the economy relative to the size of their community, even in places where they are discriminated against? Why are unemployment rates in Nordic countries relatively low despite some of the highest unemployment benefits in the world? Why do the citizens of those countries accept marginal tax rates at times in excess of 50 percent and why do those nations prosper despite record high tax rates? Why do Japanese households invest most of their savings in government debt that yields low or negative returns (in effect paying for the 'privilege' of holding that debt)? Why do Latin American countries have some of the highest rates of inequality despite tax policies that are not materially different from elsewhere? Why have African nations, with very few exceptions, systematically languished behind despite vastly different development policies?

Most of the economic literature is unable to provide an answer to these questions. The common view is that economic policies that are successful in a given location should be just as successful everywhere else. Economists typically believe that their results offer universal truths. The fact that people around the world hold different values tends to be disregarded or, at best, barely acknowledged.

There are at least three reasons for this. First, most economic theories have historically been devised in the context of western societies. For centuries, those economies were the only ones considered worthy of being studied; only after World War II did non-western economies start to warrant serious attention by economists. But even today, with economic power shifting increasingly towards Asia and, to a lesser extent, other non-western regions, economics students around the world are taught theories that predominantly originated in the West. The actions of policymakers are often guided by their western education. Many of them graduated from a western institution and firmly believe that what works in the United States (US) or the United Kingdom can readily be applied anywhere else. Countries that rely on funding from international institutions are often forced to apply policies stemming from organizations that hold the firm belief that their recommended policies apply indiscriminately to all nations.

Second, and as noted above, most economists consider market participants to act in a fully rational way. The implication is that people around the world are expected to behave and respond to incentives in the exact same way. Whilst few would argue that values are exactly the same everywhere, differences in values are considered to have little impact on economic outcomes. The logical conclusion of such a worldview is that any country can become highly developed within a few decades as long as it enacts the right policies; according to former World Bank Chief Economist Justin Yifu Lin, Burundi, which is one of the poorest countries in the world, could become another Switzerland within a generation or two.[2] This paradigm remains the foundation of most development models.

Third, even in those rare instances where economic theory involves human experiments, participants are likely to be from upscale families in the US: highly educated, young, and with a clear preference for democracy. An influential study in 2010 pointed out, "American undergraduates form the bulk of the database in the experimental branches of psychology, cognitive science, and economics."[3] Although many economic studies rely on samples that are not representative of the global population, their conclusions often imply a global reach. Most economic experiments continue to be based on feedback from undergraduate US students. This is partly due to the cost and practicality of conducting experiments with a truly global representative sample, but it is mostly due to the enduring (and erroneous) belief that conducting experiments in other countries would not significantly affect the outcome of those studies.

The belief that the same economic theories apply to every society is misleading. The same economic policies enacted in Congo, China, or Chile will often yield very different results. For reasons that will be made clear in this book, significantly reducing taxes in Nordic countries would only result in higher inequalities without spurring growth. But raising taxes in Latin American countries to levels commonly observed in Nordic countries would generate even more tax evasion and corruption without reducing in equalities. Promoting higher investments in countries that save little of their income will be largely ineffective and possibly counterproductive. Government incentives for people to start their own venture may lead to a more entrepreneurial workforce, but in Japan such efforts have failed and will continue to fail. Values also play a role in the ongoing coronavirus pandemic, as we will see in the chapter on Trust.

Whilst globalization has reduced differences in values among people around the world, it has not done so to the point where those differences no longer matter. Anyone who has traveled extensively to different countries and continents knows that values remain deeply entrenched in each of us and continue to greatly influence the way people make their decisions. In this book, we have identified four values that we believe have the greatest impact on economic life: hard work, thrift, trust towards others, and risk-taking. The first two, hard work and thrift, are dismissed by most academics (with some notable exceptions). The other two, social trust and risk preferences, have gained wider recognition over the years.

Stereotyping and National Diversity

Values are difficult to observe, measure, and interpret. When observing an individual or a group of people, we may think that they form a representative sample of an overall population and that the values they display correspond to the ones held by the wider population. The risk is to stereotype, wrongly believing that people behave in a certain way based on a few observations. The reality is that within each country, different values coexist based on factors such as socio-economic background, religion, the urban-rural divide, or other historical and cultural factors. The stereotypical Japanese is a well-dressed and stressed executive working in Tokyo. But a fisherman in Hokkaido, Japan's northern island which was largely untouched by the Japanese government until the mid-19th century, thinks and behaves quite differently from a Tokyo salaryman. A Midwesterner moving to New York may struggle to adapt to her new world, at least initially. A farmer from impoverished Gansu province in China will feel that he has little in common with a Shanghainese socialite, just as an Igbo businessman in Lagos, Nigeria will not mingle much with a Hausa laborer from remote Sokoto in the north of the country.

We need to be mindful of the diversity of values within each country. But we should also not fall into the opposite trap that these are all stereotypes and that everyone around the world shares the same values. Despite a wide range of values within each country, each population, *on average*, displays a unique set of values. The Tokyo salaryman and the Hokkaido fisherman may have their differences, but they still have much more in common than people from outside Japan: they share a common language, education, history, culture, as well as a sense of national identity. The same can be argued for the Midwesterner and the New Yorker, the Gansu farmer and the Shanghainese socialite, or the Lagos businessperson and the Sokoto laborer.

Policies

A considerable amount of work has been done over the past decades to explain different economic outcomes across nations. Most of the focus has been on *policies*, in particular how good governance, the rule of law, and democratic institutions have spurred technological progress, international trade, and a better allocation of resources. Another approach has emphasized the role of geography, such as location and climate. These works have greatly improved our understanding of why some countries have become richer than others. Much of it is reflected in this book. But the main message conveyed by this book is that some of the values associated with the citizens of each country also need to be taken into account; in fact, they should feature prominently.

Economic growth (or the lack of it) is not caused by one factor in isolation, whether that factor is a human value, a policy, or geography. If we were to assert that one single factor fully explains different economic trajectories, we would expose ourselves to countless counterexamples invalidating our claim. The emergence of single-factor theories in recent decades is probably due to over-specialization in academic circles. As economist Paul Collier put it, "[m]odern academics tend to specialize: they are trained to produce intense but narrow beams of light".[4] Stating that values such as hard work and thrift are the single most important factors for growth fails to explain why South Korea enjoys much higher living standards than North Korea, or why Chile became more prosperous than neighboring Peru. Access to the sea has made many coastal areas much more prosperous over time, but it never stopped Switzerland from becoming one of the wealthiest countries on the planet. The spectacular growth of China over the past 30 years runs counter to the argument that democratic institutions can fully explain the rise of nations.

In this book, we describe six economic policies that we believe have the greatest impact on growth: political stability, free markets, education, corruption, fiscal policies, and monetary policies. We also show how the effectiveness of those policies is often related to the human values specific to each society. Social trust should be taken into consideration when devising plans to tackle corruption and raise taxes. So should thrift when assessing the merits of an export-led economy.

The Threat of Ideology

Most of us, when forming an opinion on a specific economic matter, will first consider our prevailing ideology and ensure that our views are consistent with it. We often have a strong opinion on topics such as taxes or government regulation and we are convinced that our opinion on such matters remains valid in each and every case. But we often fail to realize that ideologies oversimplify reality and obscure our ability to think objectively. The most sensible answer that can be provided to questions such as 'Should taxes be raised?' or 'Should the government intervene?' is that *it depends*. It depends on various factors, including human values. Each economic policy should be judged on its own merits. High taxes and government intervention sometimes make sense, but other times they do not.

How often do we change our opinion when confronted with evidence of the contrary? Very rarely. We cling onto our beliefs and struggle to admit that we were wrong (and face the ensuing backlash). On the contrary, we tend to dismiss contrary evidence by discrediting it as much as possible. Surrounding ourselves with people who share our views further reinforces our beliefs. A study in 2015 asked economists a series of questions on moral issues (such as their views on fairness) and on economics. They found a strong link between the two: "Economists' substantive conclusions about the workings of the economy are suspiciously correlated with their moral values."[5] In other words, economists tend to reach the conclusions that they hope for. This tendency to stick to a prevailing ideology in turn influences the methodology used by researchers to derive their conclusions. Decisions over what to measure, over what period of time, and under what set of assumptions can greatly influence results.

No research paper, even reviewed under the most rigorous scientific process, can ever claim to be fully objective. Yet in economics, ideology plays a far too important role. Author Martin Ford describes it in these terms: "Knowing the ideological predisposition of a particular economist is often a better predictor of what that individual is likely to say than any-thing contained in the data under examination."[6] Economists and policy-makers who change their views in light of new evidence or who recognize that different circumstances call for different policies should be encour-aged, not vilified. Becoming more pragmatic and open-minded can only help us improve our understanding of how economies really work.

Limitations to Growth

This book focuses on maximizing long-term economic growth. Gross domestic product (GDP), the total value of goods and services produced in a country over a specific period of time, as well as GDP per capita, which is a country's GDP divided by its population, have been historical benchmarks of economic prosperity. Despite its wide usage, GDP has its limitations. It only accounts for paid activity, excluding unpaid work such as housework or volunteering. It measures how a nation becomes wealth-ier as a whole, but not who benefits from that wealth. Non-inclusive growth is hardly a desirable outcome if a small elite group enriches itself at the expense of the majority.

Economic growth does not always reflect increased happiness. A Japanese worker may earn a high income, but her work could entail sig-nificant levels of stress, long days at the office, little family time, and few holidays. Will she necessarily be happier than a Lagos inhabitant, known for their optimism in life despite rampant corruption and much higher poverty? Maybe not. But she does, on average, benefit from better health-care, a longer life expectancy, higher education, better financial support if she loses her job, and guaranteed pension payments. These benefits would not have been possible without economic growth. Attempts to promote happiness as a national objective and rank countries accordingly have had little success because of the inherent difficulty in measuring it.

In the above example, the Japanese worker also benefits from a cleaner environment compared to the Lagos inhabitant, but that is not to say that richer countries emit less pollution or have a better environmental track record. Economic and environmental objectives often clash, with improvements in economic growth at times occurring at the expense of our environment, especially when countries go through a phase of industrialization. The impact of economic growth on climate change and the depletion of resources that many nations rely on for their future is nevertheless beyond the scope of this book. Our focus here is firmly on economic growth and how that growth is distributed among populations.

Outline

This book is divided into two sections.

The first section explores four human values that are believed to have the greatest impact on national economic outcomes. A focus on strong work ethics in Confucian and historically Protestant societies has led those nations to become much richer, except in cases where those countries failed to adopt a market economy. We explore how thrift, among other factors, impacts savings rates around the world, and how those different savings rates have led to global imbalances. Trust plays a vital role in our lives even though we may not be aware of it, resulting in more equal societies when people generally trust each other. A lack of risk-taking has had a highly negative impact on Japan's economy in the past 30 years, and also played a major role in other developed countries struggling to emerge from a prolonged period of slow growth following the 2008 financial crisis.

The second section focuses on economic policies. Political stability, much more so than any form of governance, is a precondition for growth. So are free markets, which imply a process of creative destruction, free and fair competition, and a level playing field among individuals and companies. An educated workforce is a vital enabler of innovation and higher productivity. Corruption can seriously derail growth once it becomes endemic. Sound fiscal and monetary policies help to stabilize an economy as it goes through cycles and can greatly contribute to a more equal society as well as a more robust financial sector.

PART I
VALUES

Chapter 1

Hard Work

"They are like sulfur: insoluble."

This is how Oliveira Vianna, a Brazilian professor and jurist, had described the Japanese community in Brazil in 1932 as he presided over an immigration commission tasked with offering guidance on the future immigration policy of the country.[1] This was a time when numerous reports were drafted warning of the 'Japanese infiltration' of Brazilian society. The country's Justice Minister, criticizing the inability of Japanese migrants to blend into Brazilian society, proclaimed a few years later that Japanese "selfishness, their bad faith, their refractory character, make them a huge ethnic and cultural cyst located in the richest regions of Brazil".[2] By then, an estimated 200,000 Japanese had settled in Brazil, mostly in the state of São Paulo.

Japanese migration to Brazil really began in 1908 at a time when Brazil was facing a labor shortage in its coffee plantations, by far the country's largest export at the time. Plantations had relied heavily on slaves from Africa, but that was no longer an option after slavery had been abolished in 1888. Local authorities lured Italian, Spanish, and Portuguese migrants with generous subsidies, but the harsh reality of working in the fields led many of them to return to Europe and deterred their compatriots from migrating to Brazil.[3] Growing coffee is hard work: the plant only starts producing beans after three to five years and harvest was done exclusively by hand.[4]

Seemingly out of options, the government of São Paulo turned to an unlikely solution: Japan. Hardly any Japanese had ever set foot in Brazil, but many were keen to leave their country. Although economic prospects in Japan had improved as the nation opened to the world, growth was punctuated by frequent recessions. Rapid industrialization in the country also meant that fewer farmers were required in the fields and many of them struggled to find new jobs. The Japanese government was keen to have "low-class laborers" leave the country since "their poverty posed a national threat" at a time when Japan was trying to control the growth of its population.[5] This led poor farmers to look for better opportunities elsewhere. The United States (US) was not much of an option: it saw Japan as an aggressive and militarily powerful nation, with anti-Japanese rhetoric culminating in the 1924 Asian Exclusion Act that barred Japanese (and other Asian citizens) from entering the US. Brazil, on the other hand, was desperate to find labor for its coffee plantations and less concerned with armed conflicts on the other side of the planet.

Japanese migrants to Brazil had expected to spend just a few years in the country before returning home, but most of them would remain, initially because they could not afford to return, then because of World War II, and eventually because they were assimilating into Brazilian society.

Assimilation was far from straightforward. After the initial cultural shock, early Japanese migrants had to endure difficult working conditions and widespread discrimination. They were agricultural laborers, originating from the less educated and poorest sections of Japanese society. They struggled to venture outside their local community and converse in a language they did not understand. World War II only worsened attitudes towards the Japanese community. During the war, all Japanese publications were prohibited, schools were closed, and driving or travelling within the country required special authorization.

One would have expected that a group of lowly-educated, cash-strapped laborers heavily discriminated against and without personal connections would continue to struggle. But the Japanese never gave up. While Italian, Spanish, and Portuguese coffee laborers before them returned home, the Japanese worked hard to improve their conditions. They accumulated small savings that they invested in the education of their children. They started moving into cities, predominantly São Paulo, to set up shops. In 1958, more than half of all Japanese in Brazil worked in agriculture; today that figure has dropped to less than 10 percent.[6] They bought the cheapest land they could find and afford. This became known as *terra japonêsa* (Japanese land), "so poor in quality and so badly drained that no one else wanted it".[7] To the astonishment of the locals, after years of hard work and meticulous organization, the land began to flourish. Those who stayed in agriculture established cooperatives; they were no longer the ones picking up ripe coffee cherries.

Some Brazilians did notice the inherent qualities of Japanese workers early on. In the early 1930s, the president of the Brazilian Rural Society stated, "The Japanese are the most efficient in labor, educated, refined, sober [...] During those dark nights when the planters could not regularly pay their workers, you never saw a single impatient or complaining Japanese."[8] Such observations became the norm in the 1960s and 1970s, as Japanese Brazilians grew even more successful. Discrimination remained widespread. A common, cynical joke during those days was, "If you want to go to a good university, don't knock yourself out studying, just kill one Japanese."[9] By then, the Japanese had become a highly educated workforce.

There are currently about 1.5 million Brazilians of Japanese descent, the largest minority group in Brazil and the largest Japanese community outside Japan. The average income of Japanese Brazilians is the highest among all ethnic groups in Brazil, including White Brazilians. Japanese Brazilians earn 40 percent more than the average income of all Brazilians and 6 percent more than White Brazilians.[10]

The success of the Japanese community is not limited to Brazil. In the US, Japanese migration started in the middle of the 19th century, predominantly to Hawaii and California. More than 100,000 of them were interned in camps during World War II, not so much because of suspicious activities but solely because they were of Japanese descent.[11] As was the case in Brazil, Japanese migrants in the US were of similarly poor agricultural background, were discriminated against, and yet rose through the ranks. Their hard work made them much more productive than others: in 1981, economist Thomas Sowell wrote, "One indication of their diligence is that, when they were paid on a piece-work basis in agriculture, they earned up to twice as much as other laborers."[12] Today their average income is higher than White Americans.[13] Peru also attracted many poor Japanese migrants to its cotton and sugar plantations in the early 1900s when it faced similar labor shortages. Working conditions were appalling: a fifth of the first batch of 790 Japanese workers died within years. Discrimination was rife. In 1940, anti-Japanese riots broke out on the streets of Lima: Japanese shops were looted and burnt, and 10 Japanese-Peruvians were killed.[14] Although there are no reliable statistics on academic achievement and average income by Peruvians of Japanese descendants, they are widely believed to be highly educated and among the most economically influential ethnic communities of the country.[15] One of them, Alberto Fujimori, even became president, though his legacy is a questionable one.[16]

The remarkable rise of initially destitute Japanese in these three countries cannot be a coincidence. Put into very different societies, they eventually prospered. They did so because they shared a set of common values, among which was the willingness to work hard. It is through hard work that they achieved a better life, and if not for themselves, for the generations that followed.

More than a Stereotype

Hard work is the most controversial and sensitive human value explored in this book. It is also, in our view, the one that is the most conducive to growth. It is controversial because it is often viewed as a stereotype, a simplified vision of how people behave. We see a worker toiling for long hours or, on the contrary, idling at his workplace and might conclude that this behavior extends to an entire population. It is human nature to make inferences about an entire population based on anecdotal observations. But as we will see, this is much more than a stereotype: a hard-working population can only improve the economic prospects of a nation.

What is hard work? According to the Oxford dictionary, it is something that implies "a great deal of effort or endurance".[17] But what exactly qualifies as "a great deal of effort or endurance"? Most of us would agree that farmers who work the land 10 hours a day in scorching heat qualify as hardworking. So would a single parent juggling between her two low-paying jobs and her kids. But would a finance executive or information technology programmer who works the same number of hours a day qualify as hard-working? What about those who put "a great deal of effort or endurance" into an activity that they enjoy most of the time, such as professional athletes? If we were to ask people whether they work hard, most of them will say that they do, and few would accept to be told otherwise. Even if their activity does not involve much physical exertion, the high levels of stress that they have to deal with qualifies, in their view, as hard work.

There are many reasons why people work hard. It could be out of necessity: to feed themselves or their families. It could be ambition: accumulating wealth, attaining a higher social status, becoming famous, or leaving a mark on this world. It could be parental or peer pressure: we may work hard as children because our parents force us to, or to be part of a group if every other member of that group works hard. It could be about upholding a family's reputation. It could be linked to religious beliefs. It could be a higher, selfless motive, such as soldiers going through strenuous training to defend their country, or humanitarians working in war-torn places to help others. Out of all the possible reasons for working hard, monetary gain is probably the one that drives most people in our modern, materialistic societies.

There are also reasons why people may choose NOT to work hard. We need to be mindful here not to label people or entire communities that do not place as much emphasis on hard work as 'lazy' or other such derogatory terms. Some societies will value materialistic gains less than others. Many around the world consider family to be the most important aspect of their lives. If working long hours provides for better pay but comes at the expense of caring for family members, some of us will be less tolerant than others of such a compromise.

There is also another reason why people may wish to shun hard work. Even if they are ready to make sacrifices, they may reconsider their position if their hard work does not translate into tangible gains. The incentive to work hard will be higher in societies that promote meritocracy, create a level playing field, and fight corruption effectively, themes that will be discussed in more detail in subsequent chapters. The right policies can therefore spur workers to put extra effort into their tasks, but those workers will only act accordingly if they value the expected gains derived from their hard work above other life priorities.

Measuring Hard Work

When we think of someone who is hard-working, why do we come to such a conclusion? It could be related to the amount of time devoted to a specific activity. But it could also refer to how much work a person gets done within a specific period of time. In 1935, Alexei Stakhanov, the quintessential example of a hard-working person, became a figurehead in the Soviet Union after allegedly mining a record 102 tons of coal in a single shift of 6 hours.[18] These two measures, the amount of time spent working and how productive a person is, are common proxies for hard work.

Take the example of an artisanal baker, a profession usually associated with hard work. If the baker wakes up at 4 a.m. every morning to prepare loaves of bread and finishes his shift by 2 p.m., we may conclude that he is hard-working based on the amount of time he has spent on the job. We may reach a similar conclusion if he produces 300 loaves of bread every day when other bakers in his town only manage 200 loaves a day. The baker is more productive and therefore regarded to be more hard-working. The same conclusions can be applied to an entire economy.[19] The amount of time spent at the workplace is measured by hours worked, which is the average number of hours worked for each worker, expressed over a year. The productivity of workers is usually measured by gross domestic product (GDP) per hour worked, which considers the total production of a country within an hour.

Both measures, unfortunately, turn out to be poor indicators of hard work. People may spend a lot of time at their workplace every day, but this tells us nothing about the work that is actually done, especially in an age where many tasks can be handled without being physically present at the workplace. Office workers could be spending more time surfing the Internet, gossiping, and taking multiple coffee breaks than working on their assignments. The baker may wake up at 4 a.m. every day, but if an assistant prepares the bread and another attends to customers while he sits in a corner for hours supervising the work of his employees from time to time, he should not be considered hard-working. At the country level, aside from issues related to data sources and methods of calculation that differ in each country, part-time work heavily skews the data: Germany, commonly thought to have a hard-working population, ends up having

among the fewest hours worked in Europe largely because it has a considerable number of part-time workers. Countries where the workforce is
largely comprised of independent workers often display many hours
worked but this tells us little about how hard-working the population is:
individual shop owners must attend to their shops throughout the day but
could be spending most of those days sitting idle.

The second measure of hard work, GDP per hour worked, also suffers
from various shortcomings. As it incorporates the same measure of hours
worked in its calculation, the limitations discussed above apply to GDP
per hour worked as well. Another important shortcoming is technology.
The baker who produces more loaves of bread could have purchased new
equipment allowing him to increase productivity at minimal effort. GDP
per hour worked is more a reflection of technological progress than a
measure of hard work. Countries with the highest GDP per hour worked
are all highly developed.[20] Are workers in a country more productive
because they work harder or because they are assisted by technological
tools or better organizational methods that allow them to increase their
output? If Alexei Stakhanov really did mine 102 tons of coal within
6 hours, he would not have succeeded without improving the efficiency of
how coal was hauled from the mine and using a mining drill, a novelty at
the time.[21] The bottom line is that we do not have any economic indicator
that can provide us with a reliable measure of how hard-working a population is when comparing data between countries.

An alternative method is the use of surveys. We cannot simply ask
people directly whether they work hard, as most of them will say that they
do. The World Values Survey asks participants whether 'Hard work brings
success'.[22] But here again, there are various issues in using survey results
as a proxy for hard work. People may believe that hard work does not
bring success, but that does not in itself imply that they do not work hard.
Those who disagree the most with the statement that hard work brings
success are Haitians. They have seen their economy destroyed by years of
mismanagement and natural catastrophes; those experiences have understandably convinced many Haitians that hard work does not pay off. As for
those who do believe that hard work brings success, that does not necessarily imply that they will be willing to work hard to achieve success.

Migrating Communities

Since we struggle to measure hard work, should we simply ignore it? If we did, we would, in our view, miss a key factor as to why some nations grow faster than others. There are communities or entire countries that, on average, have populations that work harder than others. It does not always lead to higher growth: North Koreans are generally thought to be hard-working, but that has not helped them much in reaching a higher standard of living. Likewise, the collapse of the Soviet Union had little to do with the work ethics of the population of its member states. Countries with a hard-working population may be mired in poverty if other factors contributing to growth, such as the adoption of a market economy, are not implemented.

Linking hard work to economic growth implies being able to disentangle the concept of hard work from other factors affecting growth. But without a reliable metric on hard work, it is difficult to compare the work ethics of different countries. We may think that Germans are more hard-working than Greeks, but what evidence do we have to back up such a claim? Any debate about whether country A has a more hard-working population than country B will seemingly remain inconclusive because of a lack of evidence and an inability to distinguish between hard work and other factors that may facilitate or hinder growth.

This is where a study of migrating communities provides valuable insight. History is awash with waves of migration of people relocating to other countries; fleeing war, poverty, a dictatorship, or a severe economic downturn; or attracted to places with brighter prospects, in almost all cases in search of a better life. Upon arrival in their new environment, migrants, who for the purposes of this book are defined as anyone who relocates from one country to another, will in most cases be subject to the same laws, institutions, and economic policies as the rest of the population. This has not stopped some communities that were uneducated, penniless, and discriminated against from systematically, within a generation or two, managing to climb the social ladder of their adopted home and becoming even more prosperous than the local population. Their success can only be explained by the values that they were brought up with and, chief among them, their eagerness to work hard.

This has been the case for Japanese migrants in the Americas, as described in the introduction of this chapter. Their hard work has seen them rise against all odds and become one of the most successful communities in Brazil, Peru, and the US. Another better-known example is the Chinese. In every country they have migrated to, their community became highly prosperous. This cannot be a coincidence. Various accounts attest to their superior work ethics on the plantations, in factories, or at container ports.[23] There have been multiple waves of Chinese migration over centuries, starting in the middle of the 19th century. They were mostly illiterate and landless peasants, fleeing famine and war, while wealthy and educated landowners had remained in China. Throughout Southeast Asia, with the exception of Singapore, the Chinese community represents a minority: 23 percent of the population in Malaysia, 14 percent in Thailand, 3 percent in Myanmar, and 1 percent in the Philippines, Indonesia, and Vietnam.[24] Yet the wealthiest individuals and owners of large privately-owned companies are overwhelmingly ethnic Chinese. The average income of ethnic Chinese in the region is much higher than any other ethnic group.[25]

Another way to look at this is to compare the wealth of provinces of a specific country with the proportion of ethnic Chinese in those provinces, the idea being that the higher the proportion of ethnic Chinese, the wealthier the province. Malaysia is one of the few Asian countries that provides relevant data.[26] By comparing GDP per capita to the proportion of ethnic Chinese in each of the 16 Malaysian states and federal territories (Malaysia is comprised of 13 states and 3 federal territories), one finds a very strong correlation: the higher the proportion of Chinese, the higher the GDP per capita. Even excluding the capital Kuala Lumpur, which has by far the highest GDP per capita as well as the largest Chinese community, GDP per capita of rich Malaysian states is at times double or triple that of poorer states. States such as Kelantan, Perlis, Sabah, or Terengganu have the lowest proportion of Chinese and lag behind in terms of economic development, whereas the population of rich states such as Penang or Selangor is about one third Chinese. The exception is Labuan, a small federal territory near Brunei that derives most of its wealth from oil revenues and is overwhelmingly of Malay descent.[27] Every Malaysian state is governed by the same federal policies, and yet there are vastly different standards of living in each state depending predominantly on the proportion of ethnic Chinese in their population.

It is the same story in the US, where ethnic Chinese fare much better than other communities, even though many first-generation Chinese started at the bottom of the social ladder. The median income of American households of Chinese origin is 45 percent higher than the median US household income.[28] A 2012 *New York Times* article reported about an elite high school in New York City that enrolls students each year solely based on an admission test and provides free tutoring classes to prepare for the test.[29] Although Asians (mainly Chinese Americans) made up just 14 percent of the city's public-school students, they comprised 43 percent of those taking advantage of free tutoring classes. Many students of other ethnic backgrounds never bothered showing up for the tutoring classes even though they were free of charge to attend. Hard work paid off: 72 percent of successfully enrolled students were Asian Americans.

There are other examples of communities outperforming others wherever they migrate. Jews have become highly successful wherever they have resettled. Nigerians have been, on average, highly successful migrants: in the US, Americans of Nigerian descent earn more than the average American and about the same as White Americans.[30] The Basques in Latin America, the Indians in East Africa, and the Lebanese in West Africa all have a reputation for being hard-working and have, on average, done very well for themselves. It is, however, more difficult to draw firm conclusions from these cases because those migrants were often better-educated and wealthier when they reached the shores of their hosts. As such, their success could be due to hard work but also their higher initial qualifications. In the US, Indians are by far the most successful community, but they mostly represent the intellectual elite of their country, hardly a representative sample. Another challenge in reaching firm conclusions for those groups is the limited data available as only a handful of countries publish average or median income by ethnic group.

Confucian Work Ethics

We have acknowledged the challenge of comparing individual countries in terms of work ethics because of the inherent difficulty in measuring hard work and isolating it from other factors that contribute to economic growth. There are, however, clusters of countries which share similar work ethics and have systematically outperformed others over time, except when they failed to adopt a market economy. Two such clusters are Confucian and historically Protestant countries.

Countries of Confucian heritage, in which the majority of the population has followed the teachings of Chinese philosopher Confucius over centuries, have all seen exceptional growth after adopting market economies and opening up to international trade: Japan, Singapore, South Korea, and, more recently, mainland China and Vietnam. North Korea has not implemented these reforms and remains impoverished. Exceptional growth could not have materialized through market reforms alone. Other countries in the region that have implemented similar reforms (the Philippines, Indonesia, Thailand, Cambodia, Myanmar, and Laos) have enjoyed growth but nowhere to the extent of Confucian nations. An exception relates to countries that rely heavily on natural resources, such as Brunei and Malaysia, for which the oil and gas sector accounts for 65 and 30 percent of GDP, respectively.[31]

Confucian teachings emphasize the importance of hard work, education, and obedience. A person's worth is determined through merit: what he is able to achieve through his own efforts, not birthright. Hard work starts early on in life, with children spending long hours studying both at school and at home. Studies have shown that children faced with higher parental expectations tend to work harder and be more academically successful.[32] Although Confucian heritage can differ significantly between East Asian countries, the emphasis on hard work is deeply rooted in all of them. Back in 1971, Herman Kahn, an American futurist, predicted, "The Confucian ethic — the creation of dedicated, motivated, responsible, and educated individuals and the enhanced sense of commitment, organizational identity, and loyalty to various institutions — will result in all the neo-Confucian societies having at least potentially higher growth rates than other cultures."[33]

China's meteoric rise since the 1980s has been rightly attributed to markets reforms and opening up to the world, acquiring vital know-how in that process and exporting manufactured goods. These factors have indeed had an enormous impact on the Chinese economy. But they do not explain the *extent* to which China's economy has grown for more than 30 years. Many countries have implemented similar market reforms but did not witness their economy double in size every seven years or so over multiple decades. China could not have grown as much as it did without the inherent industriousness of its population.

These values were acknowledged by early visitors settling into China. Arthur Henderson Smith, an American missionary who spent more than 50 years in China from 1872 to 1926, shared his experiences in a series of books. He would marvel at the laborers and merchants who rose shortly after midnight to work in the fields and followed that up with other work, observing, "Whether it be the copper workers of Canton [Guangzhou], the tinfoil workers of Foochow [Fuzhou], the wood-carvers of Ningpo [Ningbo], the rice-mill workers of Shanghai, the cotton-cleaners and workers in the treadmill for bolting flour in the northern provinces, they may all be heard late at night, and at a preposterous hour in the morning. By the time an Occidental has had his breakfast a Chinese market is nearly over. There are few more significant contrasts than are suggested by a stroll along the bund in Shanghai, at the hour of half-past five, on a summer's morning. The lordly European, who built those palaces which line the water-front, and who does his business therein, is conspicuous by his total absence, but the Asiatic is on hand in full force, and has been on hand for a long time. It will be hours before the Occidentals begin to jostle the Chinese from the sidewalks, and to enter with luxurious ease on their round of work, and by that time the native will have finished half his day's labor."[34]

Things have evolved since those days, but not as much as we may believe. Hard work as a value has remained deeply rooted in Chinese society. Winter Nie, a professor at Switzerland's International Institute for Management Development Business School, argues, "The Chinese are simply endowed with a greater hunger for success than many Westerners, and they are ready to do whatever it takes to achieve it."[35] The '996' culture, where people work from 9 a.m. till 9 p.m. six days a week, remains the norm in many companies. Children are under a lot of pressure to succeed academically: every year, 10 million of them take part in the dreaded *gaokao*, the nationwide examination to gain admission to university. Just like anywhere else, the right incentives must be in place. If hard work produces no result, there is little incentive to persevere. Back in 1979, a journalist from *The Washington Post*, on a visit to a silk factory, reported, "As in most factories in China, workers at this [...] silk factory are not putting much effort into their work. This relaxed work attitude is going to be a major obstacle to the modernization of this most populous nation on earth."[36] When visiting factories in 1982, Harvard Professor William Overholt was equally unimpressed at the way so many workers "just stood around smoking and.chatting".[37] As the country pushed ahead with reforms after the disastrous economic policies of the 1960s and 1970s, people found another reason to work hard aside from nation-building: they could now save and accumulate wealth.

Singapore's population, which is more than 70 percent Chinese, has by and large retained its Confucian heritage. Although younger Singaporeans may not be willing to sacrifice as much as their elders did, a common generational trend throughout East Asia (and probably the rest of the world as well), hard work remains an important value guiding most Singaporeans throughout their lives. A sociologist once observed that the Singapore Chinese "on the whole consider the acquisition of wealth to be one of the most important aims in life, and almost an end in itself; they are indefatigable workers and keen businessmen".[38] The incentive to work hard is reinforced by the fact that Singapore is a highly meritocratic society, where everyone is given an equal chance to succeed. People will be more motivated to put in the effort knowing that they have a better chance of securing a stable and well-paying job if they work hard. Just like any other country, being raised in a wealthy and well-connected family does increase the likelihood of going to a better school and landing a well-paying job, but the heavy subsidization of schools and universities and the practice by public companies and government to hire workers based on merit alone ensure that social mobility in Singapore is higher compared to many other countries. A meritocratic society allows for a better allocation of human resources within the economy. It also creates a more competitive environment with students competing for the best grades and workers competing for the best jobs, raising the overall standard. If there ever was a leader who understood the importance of human values for economic growth, it was Lee Kuan Yew, Singapore's prime minister for more than

40 years, who, in 1994, stated, "We were fortunate we had this cultural backdrop, the belief in thrift, hard work, filial piety, and loyalty in the extended family, and most of all, the respect for scholarship and learning."[39]

Protestant Work Ethics

Another cluster of countries that has seen systematically stronger growth are those of Protestant tradition, which have, on average, become more prosperous than their Catholic counterparts. 15 countries are traditionally considered as historically Protestant: Germany, the Netherlands, Switzerland, Sweden, Norway, Denmark, Finland, Iceland, Estonia, Latvia, the United Kingdom, as well as those that are now mostly populated by migrants who originated from historically Protestant countries: the US, Canada, Australia, and New Zealand. Out of these 15 countries, 13 of them are ranked in the top 20 nations as measured by GDP per capita. The two exceptions are Estonia and Latvia, where economic prospects significantly deteriorated under Soviet Union rule. Since adopting market reforms, both nations have recovered and grown quickly; that trend should continue. For the sake of completeness, the seven other countries with the highest GDP per capita which are not historically Protestant are small city-states (Luxembourg, Singapore), oil producers (Qatar, the United Arab Emirates), as well as Ireland, Austria, and Belgium. Japan and South Korea are in the top 25.[40] A study by Angus Maddison of Western European nations from 1500 to 2000 concluded that countries that were predominantly Protestant generated higher GDP per capita compared to countries that were predominantly Catholic, although both sets of countries started at similar levels of economic development in the 16th century, when Protestantism emerged after the Reformation. The gap widened until 1940 and then started to converge in the 1970s (probably due to European integration). Despite this more recent convergence, a significant difference in GDP per capita remains.[41]

It cannot be a coincidence that virtually every historically Protestant country has performed better than historically Catholic ones. What caused these separate trends? The most popular yet highly controversial explanation is the one given by Max Weber, a German sociologist who published *The Protestant Ethic and the Spirit of Capitalism* in 1905. Although Weber himself did not expressly link Protestantism to economic prosperity (his focus was more on how certain aspects of Protestantism promoted modern capitalism), the common interpretation of his work has been how Protestants, because of the values they had acquired, became wealthier and saw their economies flourish. According to Weber, Catholics had little incentive to accumulate wealth. Their salvation was guaranteed as long as they submitted to the authority of the Church. Protestants adopted a very different approach when it came to the doctrine of salvation. Although there were many factions of Protestantism, they all shared a belief that hard work and materialistic success were an important step towards salvation. The pursuit of money was not a sin; on the contrary, the accumulation of wealth was encouraged. Work became a virtue, not a punishment.[42] Yet hard work was not enough: the *result* of an individual's efforts was the real proof of virtue. This is in sharp contrast to Catholicism where faith and morality alone are expected to ensure salvation. Although this schism in Christianity occurred centuries ago, the different values it generated, passed on from one generation to another, continue to play a role in contemporary societies.

Weber's theory is not very popular in academic circles. The main line of criticism is that Protestant countries performed better because of a higher focus on education and literacy, not so much because of hard work.[43] The rise in Protestantism occurred at the same time as the invention of the printing press. Education became a path to biblical understanding. Martin Luther, a seminal figure of the Reformation, felt that everyone should own a bible and read it. He encouraged his followers to build schools and learn to read for the sole purpose of understanding the words of God. At a time when more and more books were printed in Protestant countries, Catholics were forbidden from printing anything that the Church did not favor. The Roman Catholic Church was still reading the bible in Latin, which few could understand. Only clerics could teach about the Holy Scriptures.

Literacy rates are likely to have played a role in advancing Protestant economies, facilitating improved correspondence, written contracts, and bookkeeping, all of which reduced transaction costs and led to higher productivity. But if literacy rates were to be the only factor, why would differences in economic development persist to this day? Spain, Italy, and Portugal have close to a 100 percent literacy rate, yet their GDP per capita remains much lower than that of Northern European nations, with few signs of any convergence in recent decades. Most Latin American countries have very high literacy rates, yet their economies are not as developed as those in the US or Canada; in fact far from it. Protestant countries may have had a head start in increasing their literacy rates, but it has now been five centuries since the Reformation. Higher literacy rates centuries ago cannot account for contemporary differences in economic performance. The debate will never be fully settled given the difficulty in measuring hard work and the lack of reliable data back then. But the undeniable fact remains that historically Protestant nations continue to perform better, irrespective of the policies enacted in each country.

The Legacy of the Slave Trade

The greatest disincentive to hard work is when the fruits of labor do not yield any benefit to the person doing the work. An extreme example of this is slavery: a slave earns little to no income and is subjected to work under his owners. Without coercion, the slave would have no reason to do any work.

The main victim of slavery is the African continent. With an estimated 20 million Africans enslaved over a period spanning centuries, slave trade has had an enormously negative impact on Africa. The largest slave trade was the trans-Atlantic one, feeding slaves to the Americas from the 15th to the 19th century.

The impact of slavery on economic growth in Africa has been most notably studied by economist and historian Nathan Nunn.[44] Through the use of historical documents such as shipping records and looking at the ethnicity of slaves shipped on vessels, Nunn was able to observe which countries were the most affected by the slave trades and compared those observations to each country's economic performance. He found a strong link: countries that were the biggest victims of the slave trades are also the ones to have recorded the lowest growth. The Democratic Republic of the Congo, Togo, Guinea-Bissau, and Sierra Leone were among the most affected by the slave trades and are among the poorest in Africa today (and by extension, in the world). By contrast, countries such as Tunisia, Botswana, or Namibia have been mostly spared by the slave trades and achieved stronger growth. An alternative explanation is that those countries that were victims of slavery were the least developed ones to start with, even prior to the implementation of the slave trades. But Nunn shows that, in fact, it was the most developed African nations at the time that became the biggest victims of the slave trades. The impact of slavery has also been felt in countries that imported slaves. In the US, Blacks whose ancestors were not subject to slavery, such as most West Indians, have been shown to be much better educated and earn higher income compared to Blacks with an ancestry of slavery.[45]

How exactly did slavery hinder growth? Two explanations have been offered. First, slave trade prevented the formation of larger ethnic groups. This led to more ethnic diversity, impeding the development of political structures vital to economic growth. Second, with most slaves kidnapped or tricked by relatives or friends, this created an environment of mistrust; as will be discussed in a later chapter, distrust can hamper further growth.

Higher ethnic diversity often (though not always) leads to lower levels of trust among people, which would imply that the two explanations are related. Ethnic diversity and mistrust have undoubtedly played an important role in the lackluster economic performance of countries with a history of slavery. But if ethnic diversity alone were to blame, a multicultural nation such as Singapore would not have prospered. And if an absence of trust alone were to blame, Latin American nations, which display very low levels of trust, would not have seen their economies grow much faster than most African countries.

The missing explanation, in our view, is hard work. Centuries of slavery have profoundly affected people's attitude towards hard work, and this has continued long after slavery was abolished. A slave sees little value in work; on the contrary, it is associated with exploitation. Writer Carlos Rangel observed, "A number of factors inhibit the development of societies based on slavery: the passive resistance to work that is the earmark of the slave; the absurd prestige of idleness that afflicts his master; and [...] a rhythm of life so little concerned with punctuality."[46] In countries that supplied slaves, people had little incentive to work hard knowing that at any moment in time, their belongings could be confiscated and their freedom lost if they had the misfortune to be forced onto ships to a faraway land and a very bleak future. This negative attitude towards work, inherited from centuries of abuse by slave masters, has persisted to this day.

A Higher Growth Potential

Countries that tried to import better work ethics from elsewhere have found that human values cannot simply be transmitted over a short period of time. It takes generations to acquire them. Malaysia's leader over two decades, Mahathir Mohamad, is a great admirer of East Asian economies, in particular Japan. He would observe how those economies prospered through hard work, discipline, and strong management. He saw how successful the Chinese minority in Malaysia had become and would often lament the fact that Malays had little motivation to work hard, often relying on state support. As part of his 'Look East' policy, Malay students and trainees were sent to Japan to learn about Japanese values and expertise in the hope that those values would permeate Malaysian society and herald a new era of continued growth. That did not happen. Malays prioritize strong family ties over the accumulation of wealth or economic power. Technology transfers have also failed to materialize.

It is our firm belief that the population of certain societies, on average, work harder than others. The systematic success of Japanese and Chinese overseas communities has been achieved through effort and perseverance. Hard work does not always translate into higher economic growth, but it provides for higher *potential* growth. A developing country endowed with a hard-working population and the implementation of the right economic policies has the potential to, and in all likelihood will, transform itself into a highly developed nation within a generation or two. But societies with a population that shuns hard work will struggle to join the ranks of prosperous nations. They could put in place all the right policies, but policies alone will not suffice. A lack of hard work effectively creates a ceiling above which an economy will not be able to grow further. An exception to this rule is nations with substantial natural resources and the ability to manage those resources well.

Chapter 2

Thrift

"Whatever else he might be, Germany's Mr. Average is very good at not spending money. He makes sure he squeezes the very last dollop of toothpaste out of the tube, and sometimes he'll even cut it in half with a pair of scissors so as not to waste anything. He teaches his children exactly how hard to press down on the liquid soap dispenser to avoid using up too much. He never leaves the lights on; he turns the shower tap off while he lathers his hair and he always uses his tea bags twice."[1]

The Germans are well-known for their thriftiness and their abhorrence of debt. German households save about 10 percent of their disposable income, twice as much as the average European Union household.[2] What motivates Germans to save more has little to do with their economic prospects. If that were the case, we would expect large fluctuations over the years as the country goes through bouts of economic booms and busts. Instead, savings rates have remained remarkably stable over time. During the boom years preceding the global financial crisis, Germans did not incur more debt or increase their spending. Even with most of their savings wiped out three times during the 20th century, following two world wars and one of the worst cases of hyperinflation ever recorded, Germans patiently rebuilt their personal finances by saving a high portion of their income.

Germans are taught the importance of thrift from a young age. The country's savings banks, which are legally mandated to promote saving, regularly visit local schools to teach the virtue of thrift. Every year towards the end of October, Germany is one of a handful of countries still celebrating World Thrift Day, where children deposit the savings they have accumulated to the bank. Germans have been savers for centuries. The origins of their thriftiness can be traced back to the end of the 18th century, when the first savings bank was created. Numerous others followed: by 1900, more than eight million savings accounts existed in what was known at the time as Prussia.[3] By then, Protestant tradition had made it a virtue to renounce present satisfaction for future gains.

Thrift and Saving Behavior

Similar to hard work and other human values explored in this book, thrift, commonly defined as the careful use of money, is a value that people acquire to varying degrees, mostly developed throughout childhood. The children of thrifty parents have been shown to display similar levels of thrift as their parents even when their income is materially different from that earned by their parents.[4] Our attitude towards thrift seldom changes over time: if we are thrifty as teenagers or young adults, we usually remain so throughout our lives.

A related but different concept to thrift is the savings rate of individuals or households, which measures how much of our disposable income we set aside; in other words, what is not spent (or 'consumed'). If our monthly disposable income is $1,000 and we are left with $100 by the end of the month, our savings rate is 10 percent. Each individual or household has its own savings rate, with some of us saving more and others less. Adding up the savings rates of every household in a country yields the national household savings rate, which is the proportion that each household, on average, saves from their income.[5]

Many factors affect savings rates. People save to better prepare for future expenditures such as medical bills, school fees, retirement, a marriage, children, the repayment of a debt, a new car, a luxury handbag, or a holiday. At an older age, we may wish to save to leave a bequest. Income levels make a difference: people with a higher income tend to save more.

Life expectancy, the number of children we have, wealth, the current state of the economy, social security systems, tax systems, inflation, interest rates, the government's future fiscal policy, financial markets, and education levels are all likely to play a role as well.

Few economists would include thrift in this list, believing that it plays no role, or at best a marginal one, in determining the savings rates of people. Societies around the world have very different personal savings rates: Chinese households save a lot more than American ones. But are these differences related to thrift or some of the other factors described above? The difficulty is to disentangle the various possible causes to understand which ones have the greatest impact on savings rates.

One way to assess the possible impact of thrift on personal savings rates is to look at survey data. The World Values Survey asks participants whether thrift is a quality that children should be encouraged to learn at home. By comparing the proportion of people who view thrift as an important quality to each country's national savings rate out of a sample of 53 countries, a strong correlation emerges: countries where people view thrift as an important value to teach children end up with higher savings rates.[6]

Another approach is to observe the saving behavior of migrants in a specific country and compare that to the savings rate prevalent in the country of their ancestors. If migrants, especially second or third-generation ones, have a very different savings rate than the local population but one which is similar to their country of origin, this tells us that institutional factors cannot be the only explanation. If Chinese migrants established for decades in the United States (US) continue to save a much higher portion of their income compared to American households of similar income levels, the logical conclusion is that their attitudes towards saving remain firmly ingrained in their mindset.

For many years, that debate seemed to have been settled. A 1994 study focusing on migrants in Canada found no difference in savings rates between the various countries of origin of migrants. That study suffered from several shortcomings, acknowledged by the authors: the country of origin only referred to five regions, not specific countries (China, for example, was bundled together with Southeast Asia) and the sample sizes were small, in some cases amounting to just 150 migrants per region.[7] The authors looked to address these shortcomings in a new study in 1998, this time focusing on the US. They found significant differences in savings rates depending on the origin of migrants as measured by their country of birth, but could not tie those savings rates with the country of origin. For example, Italian, Greek, or Portuguese migrants in the US were found to have higher savings rates than Chinese or Korean migrants even though savings rates in Italy, Greece, or Portugal were much lower than in China or South Korea. Although not the conclusion of the authors, this was taken as evidence that thrift or other values played no or little role in determining personal savings rates.

What many failed to realize at the time is that the US does not provide data on personal savings rates by origin or ethnic group. The 1998 study calculated those savings rates by comparing the average wealth of households in the 1980 Census to that in the 1990 Census, using the difference in wealth as a proxy for savings. This is questionable because within a span of 10 years, the population of migrants within each ethnic group would have changed significantly, with migrants of varying wealth levels entering and leaving the country. Even the wealth component had to be approximated as it was not available in the census. Financial wealth, calculated as the capitalized value of interest and dividend income, was added to the net value of housing owned by each household. The market value of housing was included in the census, but not the mortgage, which had to be estimated as well. A clear evidence of the inadequacy of this methodology is that US-born households, which comprised 92 percent of the overall US population at the time, were estimated to have a savings rate that was less than half the actual savings rate in the country.[8]

More recently, further studies have observed second-generation migrants in countries where data on savings rates by country of origin is readily available. One study in 2017 focused on Germany and found that the savings rates of second-generation migrants from 69 different countries were strongly correlated to the savings rates of the country of their ancestors.[9] In other words, even after living in Germany for decades, migrants retained the savings behavior prevalent in their country of origin.[10] Another study in 2018 that looked at first, second, and third-generation migrants in the United Kingdom (UK) found similar results.[11] Chinese migrants to the UK save a substantial portion of their income, in line with savings rates in

China, whereas those from Ghana, for example, save very little, even at similar income levels. The correlation remains strong even for third-generation migrants, despite them being subject to the exact same institutional factors as the rest of the population. What these studies show is that thrift is an important factor in the savings behavior of people, much more so than is commonly believed.

Private Versus National Savings

Individuals are not the only ones saving; businesses and governments save as well. Net profits generated by the operations of a business over a specific period, less dividends and taxes, divided by revenue, represents the savings rate of a company. Governments run surpluses or deficits depending on whether their revenues are higher or lower than public expenditure. Combining the savings of all three economic actors (households, businesses, and governments) of a specific country and comparing that to the country's total income (its gross domestic product (GDP)) yields the national or gross savings rate, which reflects how much a country saves in aggregate.[12] A national savings rate of 20 percent implies that households, businesses, and the government *collectively* save 20 percent of their income; in other words, everything that a country produces less what it consumes.[13] When it comes to the workings of an economy, national savings rates, as opposed to household saving rates, are the preferred indicator because they represent the overall savings made by all market participants. Data for national savings rates is also more readily available and more reliable than household savings rates, especially in developing countries.

Thrift is unlikely to play much of a role in determining the savings rates of businesses, which in their vast majority aim to maximize profits. As for governments, countries with high personal savings rates often have the highest government savings. Each year, the countries that record a government surplus are mostly those with high household savings rates and traditionally considered thrifty: Norway, Liechtenstein, Iceland, Sweden, New Zealand, Germany, the Netherlands, South Korea, Luxemburg, and Switzerland.[14] It would therefore appear that policymakers who are thrifty with their personal finances are also thrifty when managing the finances of a country. German policymakers are well-known for their fiscal discipline and become uncomfortable whenever public deficits soar, a sentiment shared by most of their fellow citizens. This was the case after reunification when the country spent vast amounts on infrastructure in the ex-East Germany, and again following the 2007–2008 financial crisis. On each occasion, one of the main priorities of policymakers was to rebalance their public finances. The structural deficit of the federal government is limited to 0.35 percent of GDP by law, with the country systematically aiming for 'die schwarze Null', that is, a balanced budget. Whilst this policy is at times criticized for treating public finances in a similar way as private household finances, it remains popular among the majority of Germans. Nordic countries, Switzerland, Taiwan, and Singapore are also known for their fiscal discipline.

Thrift therefore plays *some* role in determining national fiscal balances. We should, however, also be cognizant of a few observations. First, rich countries are mainly the ones running public surpluses. Even if policymakers in poor countries wanted to balance their budget, they would often not be in a position to do so, constrained by limited revenues. Second, there are countries with thrifty populations (or at least with high household savings rates) which end up running large public deficits, such as Japan. Third, and perhaps most importantly, managing the finances of a country is very different from managing personal finances. A balanced fiscal budget could come at the expense of households or companies and have a detrimental impact on the economy. If the government significantly increases taxes or reduces spending, citizens and businesses may feel the pinch and decide (or be forced) to reduce their consumption and investment. Governments should aim to strike the right balance between fiscal discipline and growth.

Thrift is therefore likely to play a role in national savings rates, but predominantly at the household level, which often forms a significant portion of national savings rates. We do not know the extent to which thrift impacts national savings rates compared to other factors. But dismissing thrift entirely, as is typically done, prevents us from truly understanding why large differences in savings rates between nations persist over time, irrespective of the policies adopted by those nations.

Savings Rates Around the World

East Asian and Northern European countries display the highest national savings rates in the world. China saved 46 percent of its income in 2018, Singapore 53 percent, and South Korea 35 percent. Japan is noticeably lower at 27 percent, though still high by international comparison. Norway saved 36 percent of its GDP, the Netherlands 32 percent, Sweden 30 percent, Denmark 29 percent, Germany 29 percent, and Finland 23 percent.[15] Also having very high savings rates are nations endowed with large natural resources which have managed those resources well: Brunei (56 percent of national savings), Qatar (48 percent), Botswana (37 percent), Algeria (38 percent), and Kuwait (35 percent). These countries do not have high personal savings rates but the strong revenues they generate from their natural resources allow them to save a large portion of their national income (in these cases, thrift plays no role).

Savings rates have historically been higher in Protestant and Confucian societies, both of which emphasize the importance of delaying present consumption for future enjoyment. A 2013 worldwide study asked participants to choose between the certainty of receiving $3,400 this month or $3,800 the following month.[16] The implied annualized interest rate is 280 percent, making the second option much more attractive. 90 percent of Germans and more than 75 percent of Scandinavians chose to wait and pocket the extra return. But only 43 percent of Italians, 47 percent of Greeks, and 48 percent of Spaniards chose to wait; a majority of respondents from these countries would rather cash in $3,400 right away than wait an extra month for a higher payout. Those most reluctant to wait an extra month were the Nigerians: only eight percent of them chose to wait.[17]

Chinese households are traditionally considered to be thrifty and save about 40 percent of their income, one of the highest rates in the world. Another factor that is likely to have had an impact on higher savings rates since the 1980s is the one-child policy, for two separate reasons. One is that families with one child have less expenditure and are therefore able to save more. The other reason is that with fewer children, parents are likely to receive less financial and physical support during old age and decide to save more as a result. Taha Choukhmane of Yale University provided convincing evidence that the one-child policy led to higher savings rates. Together with his colleagues, using survey data, they compared the savings rates of families with twins to those with only one child and found that households with twins saved about 10 percentage points *less* than households with one child, a significant difference.[18] Having fewer babies does not systematically lead to higher savings rates: many countries have seen their fertility rates drop but their savings rate did not increase. But in China, the drastic reduction in children per household at the end of the 1970s (from three to one) has led to higher savings.

Willingness Versus Ability to Save

Savings rates tend to be lower in poorer countries. The Chinese saved very little under Mao Zedong at a time when China was one of the poorest nations on Earth. They did not suddenly become thriftier after China enacted its reforms under Deng Xiaoping. They were just as thrifty under Mao as they are today, but they could not *afford* to save. People in poor countries may want to save a certain portion of their income, but they are unable to do so because of their low income and the need to purchase basic necessities such as food, clothing, and shelter that represent a higher portion of their income compared to those living in wealthier nations. Although no reliable data exists, North Korea probably has a very low savings rate despite a thrifty population.

If North Korea's prospects were to improve, savings rates would undoubtedly rise as people's ability to save increases. As China grew richer, people and businesses were able to save an increasing portion of their income. Countries that become richer typically see an increase in savings. A study of 62 countries between 1967 and 1995 shows that domestic savings rates increase with income, but as income increases, savings increase at a lower rate.[19] As far as personal savings rates are concerned, there comes a point where the *actual* savings rate aligns with the *desired* savings rate, at which savings rates no longer increase.

Thrift as a human value tells us about the willingness to save, reflected in the average *desired* savings rate specific to each society. Whether we actually reach that desired savings rate depends on our ability to do so, which in turn depends on income levels. Fast-rising economies witness an increase in their savings rate as people, and also businesses and governments, are able to save a higher portion of their income.

That is not to say cyclical or structural factors do not play a role in adjusting savings rates. Households and businesses in the US, the UK, Canada, and Australia all reduced their savings rate in the mid-2000s because of low interest rates that made it cheaper to borrow but also because of high confidence in economic prospects at the time. During an economic downturn, people and businesses become more cautious. They end up consuming and investing less (and therefore saving more, as long as their income levels are not reduced). Cyclical changes in interest rates, inflation, and taxes, among other factors, all affect savings decisions, at least temporarily.

Cyclical or structural policies that adjust the relative proportion of income of households, companies, and governments as a share of GDP can also affect national savings. Germany saw a large increase in its national savings rate from 22 percent in 2000 to 29 percent in 2018. This had nothing to do with German households becoming thriftier: they continued to save 10 percent of their disposable income. It had much more to do with Germany introducing labor reforms in the early 2000s that caused wages to grow at a much slower pace.[20] As a result, household income as a share of GDP decreased. Since households save 10 percent of their disposable income and the state 'saves' very little, most national saving in the country is done by local businesses. Those companies ended up saving more because wages stagnated at a time when the economy was booming, causing the national savings rate to increase. A similar scenario played out in China from 2000 to 2010, where a sharp increase in the national savings rate was mostly due to higher savings generated by corporates and the government (household savings also increased during the period, but not as much). Because wages had not kept up with the country's productivity gains, Chinese companies, both public and private, were able to save a much higher portion of their income, which also resulted in higher tax revenues for the state.

Too often, though, cyclical or structural factors are used to justify prevailing savings rates. China's exceptionally high household savings rate is often attributed to weak social benefits. Deprived of their iron rice bowl, Chinese households, as the story goes, are required to save more to cover for unemployment, medical expenses, retirement, and other expenses. There are, however, countless examples that invalidate such an argument. According to that line of reasoning, the US, or the UK, where the welfare state is weaker than in continental Europe, should have much higher savings rates compared to continental Europe, and yet the opposite is true. Some countries have excellent welfare support but continue to save much of their income. Sweden and Switzerland, which have some of the best social security systems in the world, are among the highest savers. China, Sweden, and Switzerland have high savings rates in part because their people are inherently thrifty and are able to save as much as or close to what they would want to save. Cyclical and structural factors do play a role as well, but they are not the primary reason for the high savings rates observed in those nations.

Savings, Investments, and Exports

Savings do not just remain idle. They eventually make their way into investments, assets that are used for future consumption (factories, equipment, machinery, and increasingly research and intellectual property). Not all investments end up being productive: building bridges to nowhere, ghost cities, or digging holes and refilling them may help an economy recover from a severe recession by providing jobs for the unemployed, but it is hardly a recipe for sustained growth. Banks play a vital role in this process by channeling the savings of individuals and businesses into investments. Countries with higher savings rates will typically have higher investment rates.

Not all domestic savings end up in domestic investment and not all domestic investment is financed via domestic savings. In an open economy, investments will also be financed through funding from abroad and local savings will also finance foreign investments. Countries that save more, by definition, consume less. Faced with lower domestic demand, businesses must find buyers outside their national borders to sell the goods and services they produce if they want to expand further. Conversely, countries with low savings rates, and therefore high consumption rates, will attract foreign funding, with local companies focusing more on their domestic market. That may not be sufficient to satisfy the high local demand for goods and services, enticing foreign companies to enter the local market (if they are allowed and able to do so). As a result, countries with high savings rates tend to export more than they import, whilst the opposite is true for countries with lower savings rates. According to the latest available figures, out of 24 countries with a national savings rate above 30 percent, 15 of them (or 63 percent) were net exporters. This is quite a high number considering that only a third of all 194 nations are net exporters.[21] There were only nine countries with the unusual combination of high national savings rates (above 30 percent) and net imports: India, Bangladesh, Sri Lanka, Nepal, the Philippines, Algeria, Malta, Ethiopia, and Macedonia. This reflects a situation where domestic investments are even higher than domestic savings. This is unusual because we would expect local companies to be much more active in export markets. The reasons that can explain this discrepancy include restrictions in the size of companies, meaning that few of them will be large enough to compete internationally; complicated procedures to export that reduce the incentive to do so; the impact of remittances; and the use of offshore finance centers primarily for tax purposes.

The point here is that, given a few exceptions, countries with high savings rates will end up with high investment rates and net exports, exporting their *excess* savings over investments at home. Countries with low savings rates usually end up saving less than what they invest at home and have to make up for the difference by borrowing from abroad (or selling assets to foreign entities) and running current account deficits.[a] These different structures have deep policy implications, one of which is the growing gap between thrifty and less thrifty nations that inevitably leads to global imbalances.

Global Imbalances

Thriftville and Squanderville are two islands of equal sizes, located next to each other. They both start out by being self-sufficient with food, the

[a]The current account represents the balance of imports and exports of goods and services, as well as a few other more minor items. By definition, the difference between domestic savings and domestic investments will be the current account balance.

only item produced. Over time, the people of Thriftville decide to save more, increasing their food production. Now that they have more food than they need, they export the surplus to Squanderville in exchange for bonds, a promise to pay for the food at a later stage. The Squanders can hardly believe their luck: they are getting food without having to work for it. At some point, the Thrifts begin to question the ability of Squanders to repay those bonds when they mature. So instead of asking for further bonds, they start to buy Squanderville land; after all, Squanderville is more likely to default on the bonds than to confiscate the land acquired by the Thrifts. Ultimately, the current generation of Squanders end up obtaining all the food they require at minimal effort, but they also put a heavy toll on future generations of Squanders, who will have to deal with the aftermath of repaying their economy's mounting debt.

Though highly simplified, this scenario described by Warren Buffet in a 2003 article for *Fortune* magazine, referring to China and the US, illustrates the potential consequences when countries end up with excess savings that are absorbed by other nations. Despite its rising external debt, it is unlikely for the US to find itself in a situation where its ability to repay its debt becomes a legitimate concern, given the fundamental strength of the US economy and the dominance of the US dollar in international trade. But its relatively low savings rate combined with the emergence of high-saving countries such as China and Japan have resulted in an imbalance as these countries, in an effort to keep their exchange rate low, channel their excess savings to the US by purchasing government bonds, reducing long-term interest rates that serve as a basis for mortgages and other long-term borrowings. These abnormally low long-term rates, which under normal circumstances fall outside the control of central banks, provided an incentive for US consumers to take on additional debt at a lower cost. To a large extent, Chinese savers ended up funding the debt that American consumers were eager to take on. The subprime crisis had multiple origins, but low long-term interest rates were an important factor in the piling up of ever-increasing amounts of debt.

Savings imbalances were also at play in Europe. High savings rates in Germany coupled with lower wages (because of the labor reforms described earlier) and competitive German industries contributed to large trade surpluses. As a member of the eurozone, Germany was unaffected by currency appreciation which would have made its exports less competitive. German excess savings found their way into other countries, including Southern European nations, leading those nations to borrow ever-larger sums. The 2010 European crisis pitted a 'frugal' North, mainly comprised of Germany, reluctant to bail out a 'spendthrift' South unless those countries made concrete efforts to balance their books. Spending habits are hard to change: a decade later, as the coronavirus pandemic forced European Union leaders to negotiate a European stimulus package, the same North/South divide emerged.

One cannot blame high-saving countries for structuring their economies based on the thriftiness of their population. China and Germany have every right to export their excess savings. Just as the Squanders in Buffett's article realized too late, it is for policymakers in countries with lower savings rates to manage their economies despite global imbalances that are here to stay. This entails adequate regulation of foreign savings channeled into the country and also better protection for local consumers whose lack of thrift can lead them to binge on debt.

Ageing Populations and the Rise of Consumerism

Two trends are having long-term consequences on savings rates around the world.

The first can be found in demographics. Many rich countries are seeing their savings rates decrease not because their citizens are becoming less thrifty, but because their populations are ageing and their retirees are unable to save as much as they would like to. Those in retirement have to make do with pensions that are at times much lower than the income they used to earn, meaning that their level of basic consumption represents a larger portion of their income. They would want to save more, but are unable to. This is especially true of Japan and South Korea, two of the fastest ageing societies. Although national savings rates remain relatively high in both countries, they have been steadily declining. Individuals in particular have seen their savings rates drop. Both countries had some of the highest household savings rates in the world back in the 1970s and 1980s, with households saving around a quarter of their income. Nowadays they save much less: South Korean households save less than

10 percent of their income, Japanese households less than 5 percent.[23] This is not because South Korean and Japanese citizens have become less thrifty. The overall household figures mask a stark contrast between generations. Young and middle-aged South Koreans and Japanese continue to save significant portions of their income in line with how they value thrift. But an increasingly high number of retirees are unable to save. Japanese citizens under 60 years old continue to save a quarter of their disposal income, whereas those over 60 have negative savings rates, effectively depleting their accumulated wealth.[24] State pensions in Japan and South Korea are low compared to other OECD (Organisation for Economic Co-operation and Development) nations despite high living costs. In both countries, state pensions are often complemented with financial support from family members.[25]

Standard economic theory argues that individuals, acting rationally, discount the expected value of their future earnings to determine what portion of their income they should save throughout their lifetime (and possibly beyond, in the form of a bequest). Younger individuals, as the theory goes, save little and take on more debt as they anticipate that their future higher income will allow them to repay those debts. As they grow older, they repay their debt and save a higher portion of their income. As they get closer to retirement, their life expectancy is reduced, they run down their assets and save less. When we look at countries such as the US, Japan, or South Korea, we observe that ageing populations coincide with lower savings rates, leading some to conclude that lower savings rates among retirees are the result of a lower incentive to save. Yet the theory does not hold in countries where citizens enjoy comfortable pensions. Germany, Switzerland, Austria, and the Nordic countries all have rapidly graying populations but have kept relatively high savings rates (both at the national and household levels). Retirees in these countries continue to save as much as they did throughout their lifetime, in line with the way they value thrift, because they are *able* to do so. Retirees in Japan or South Korea do not save less because they have fewer years to live; they save less because they cannot *afford* to save more. In China, the household savings curve is u-shaped, with younger and older households saving more than the middle-aged, which is exactly the opposite of what standard economic theory would suggest. The Chinese usually live with their families until they get married and have their parents pay for their studies. When they start a job, they will have few expenses, if any. Because they are inherently thrifty, they save most of their income. Throughout their lives, they would rather continue to save a high portion of their income, but as they get married and move out of the family house, costs start to accumulate: a property, children, maybe a car. They feel a duty to financially support their elders who often live under the same roof. These expenses prevent them from saving as much as they would like to despite rising income levels. As they go into retirement, their children become financially independent and provide them with financial support, allowing retirees to increase their actual savings rate closer to the rate they desire.

The other long-term or structural trend affecting savings rates is the rise of consumerism: the tendency to consume an ever-increasing portion of income which has pushed savings rates lower. In 1930, economist John Maynard Keynes published an essay entitled *Economic Possibilities for our Grandchildren*, in which he imagined how life could be a hundred years later.[26] He predicted that living standards would be eight times higher, allowing people to accumulate wealth and work not more than three hours a day. It turns out that Keynes was remarkably accurate about higher living standards. Real (inflation-adjusted) income per person increased 5.6 times in the US from 1930 to 2010.[27] We earn 5.6 times more (again, in real terms) than our ancestors did 80 years ago.

But what Keynes did not anticipate is that we do not have more savings. We earn much more, but we also spend more. A 2010 study showed that "the median US working-age family held less than one month's income in cash, or in checking, savings, or money-market accounts". Another study from 2005 found that in the UK, "expenditures are down a full 18 percent in the last week of the monthly pay period, relative to expenditures in the first week after payday".[28] Despite much higher income levels, the average worker has the same financial difficulties as his ancestors did decades ago.

How did this happen? In a consumerist society, a higher income creates greater 'needs' for most people. Today many of us 'need' to have the latest smartphone, fancy holiday escapades, or expensive dinners. Expenses are often a secondary concern when it comes to these special moments in life: the average wedding in the UK costs around US$35,000, about the same as the average annual income in the country.[29] Some of these spending decisions are motivated by the desire, and sometimes the need, to display a higher social status, a sign of 'conspicuous consumption'.

In our market economies, businesses tend to exploit our psychological weaknesses and our ignorance to trick us into various purchases, whether they relate to consumer goods, houses, or complex financial products. That is not to say that free markets are a bad thing, in fact far from it. But left unregulated, they lead to excesses, as the global financial crisis has made all too clear. A major reason why people, and particularly those with fewer qualifications, end up overspending is a lack of education in personal finance. A survey showed that only 60 percent of Americans understood that if their savings account returns one percent a year but inflation is two percent a year, their money after one year would buy less than it does today.[30] During the boom years of 2002–2007, people were fulfilling their dream of purchasing a home despite no or little income, attracted by the absence of a down payment and teaser rates but oblivious to the financial burden that their mortgage payments would create a few years down the road. Regulations are needed to protect those who are most vulnerable. The sophistication of financial markets in Anglo-Saxon countries, which provides easier access to credit for many households (as opposed to bank-dominated economies in continental Europe), also explains why the trend towards lower savings rates is more pronounced in the US or the UK despite their Protestant heritage. Consumerism is taking hold in other places as well, including bastions of thrift. In China and India, frugal older generations watch in disbelief as their children or grandchildren spend an ever-increasing portion of their income.

Self-control

The rise of consumerism reflects ever more ingenious ways by businesses to get people to spend more, but it also reflects a lack of self-control. Most people understand that they should not spend as much as they do, that they should save more for their older days, but too often, they lack the willpower to do so. Offering more money to them or cancelling their debt will not solve the issue. People eventually fall back to the same old habits. In the Philippines, an experiment was conducted in which all the debt of a sample of low-income individuals was fully repaid; almost all of them eventually fell back into debt.[31] Debt cancellation can help, but debt cancellation alone will not increase savings if the causes of a lack of savings are not properly addressed.

One way to increase savings is to force people to save more, for example by forcing them to contribute higher amounts into retirement accounts. Switzerland, Australia, and many others mandate private pension coverage.[32] Another solution is to offer citizens a new, attractive alternative. In the early 1980s, when Chile offered its people to opt out of the state pension system into a private one in which they could track their contributions, the response was enthusiastic and over time resulted in the highest national savings rate in Latin America.[33] A more subtle way to get people to save more is to nudge them. In the US, automatically enrolling workers into retirement schemes whilst still giving them the option to opt out raised participation levels from 10 to 80 percent.[34] Automatically increasing contributions as income rises similarly results in much higher contributions. People just do not follow these matters as closely as they should.

In developing countries, self-control is also about access to bank accounts. Despite significant improvements in the past decade, only 35 percent of those living in sub-Saharan countries hold a bank account.[35] When savings are stored under a mattress, within physical reach, the temptation to spend it is that much greater (and so is the risk of having it stolen). If the money runs out, this is often rationalized by the fact that this can always be compensated by working a bit harder, taking a side job, or requesting a loan from a friend.

Opening a bank account in poor countries is not as easy as it may seem. Banks can be expensive and are often not keen to have low-income workers open accounts with small balances that incur higher administrative fees. Some banks require minimum account balances, or they could be inaccessible from where people live. The documentation needed to open an account may not be well understood by those with little education or might simply be unavailable (not everyone holds identity papers). Some will also struggle to trust banks with safekeeping their savings. And yet, having a bank account does make a difference. In Uganda, people holding a new bank account had saved 3 times more within 12 months than those without one.[36] Similar results were found elsewhere in the world.[37]

The solution may well come from technology. Increasingly, banks are being bypassed. Mobile phone payments and accounts are becoming more popular. A fifth of sub-Saharan Africa's population is now believed to have an account linked to a mobile phone.[38] Within a decade, the region has become a global leader in 'mobile money', particularly in East Africa.[39] Abhijit Banerjee and Esther Duflo are part of a rare breed of academic economists who explore the world to see how it really works. In *Poor Economics*, they describe various ingenious ways that the poor use to improve their self-control on savings, for example by having acquaintances manage their savings. They also describe how some people take loans at prohibitive rates and deposit them in savings accounts so that it gives them the discipline to save for a special event, such as the dowry of a daughter. These are small nudges, but they can make a big difference in saving patterns.[40]

Chapter 3

Trust

After recording its first coronavirus case on March 5, 2020, South Africa reacted swiftly. Within 10 days, schools were shut, national borders closed, and large gatherings prohibited. By March 27, the country had entered a nationwide lockdown, one of the strictest in the world. Outdoor exercise was banned, and so were sales of alcohol and tobacco. One man was charged with attempted murder for breaching regulations by going to work and contaminating others. Heavy fines were meted out. More than 70,000 army troops were deployed in the streets to enforce the lockdown. Yet despite these drastic measures, and to the surprise of many observers, the number of new cases and deaths continued to rise. Official figures show that, by the end of September 2020, the country had recorded almost 700,000 cases and 17,000 deaths.

Thailand also imposed a lockdown at around the same time, a softer version that allowed people to exercise outdoors. The Southeast Asian nation has a similar population size, standard of living, and number of persons per household as South Africa. But it was much more successful at fighting the pandemic. By the end of September 2020, Thailand had recorded just 3,600 cases and 59 deaths. The numbers are probably under-reported in both countries, but it makes no doubt that Thailand has done a better job at keeping the virus at bay.

South African policymakers are not alone in scratching their heads as to why their approach did not yield the expected results. Peru also reacted quickly in implementing a strict lockdown. Yet the virus continued to spread, with Peru recording as many deaths per capita as Brazil, a country that did not impose a nationwide lockdown. In fact, all countries in Latin America have struggled to contain the virus, whatever the policies they put in place. At the other end of the spectrum, Japan did not implement a strict lockdown. The government merely recommended its citizens to take precautions. People were free to follow those guidelines or to ignore them. Most continued to commute to work. There were no penalties imposed. The country did very little testing, only doing so on those cases presenting the most severe symptoms. Despite a population twice as large as South Africa and much older, and so more at risk, Japan recorded only a fraction of all cases and fatalities compared to South Africa.

Lockdowns, however painful they may be, were essential in most countries to prevent the spread of the virus, together with other measures such as the wearing of masks and contact tracing. But these various measures do not fully explain why some nations failed to control the virus outbreak despite enforcing strict measures, whilst others had a much lighter approach and still escaped relatively unscathed. What we too often fail to take into account is the behavior of people and how that behavior differs around the world. Measures to contain the virus can only be effective if people actually comply with those measures. Most people do, but a minority will not. In some countries, that rebellious minority can be a sizable one and impede the efforts of local authorities, with devastating effects on livelihoods and economies. In Thailand and Japan, the vast majority of the population diligently followed rules and guidelines. But in South Africa, a staggering 230,000 people were charged for breaching lockdown restrictions.[1] In most of Europe and the United States (US), authorities urged individual responsibility, exhorting their citizens to comply with social distancing and limiting outdoor activities. But within days, large crowds were flocking to parks or beaches to enjoy the sunny weekends.

Why did people in different countries behave so differently? To a large extent, this is the result of the trust we have in others. If we trust others to do the right thing, we will also do our part. But if we do not trust others, we will fail to consider how our behavior could impact them.

Wearing masks is a typical example: most masks do not protect the person who wears one, but protects those whom we come in close contact with. If everyone wears a mask, we are all better protected. But if there is no trust in others, people will see little use in wearing their own mask. As of the time of writing, every nation with a high proportion of trust in others, with the notable exception of Sweden, has been successful in curbing the spread of the virus.[2]

The Merits of Trust

Trust plays a vital role in our lives even though we may not be aware of it. When we think of trust, we usually associate it with people: we place different levels of trust in our family members, our friends, our neighbors, even people we have never met before. There are entire professions that we trust more than others: doctors, for example, are more trusted than insurance brokers. There are also companies or brands we trust more: supermarket chains are typically more trusted than internet service providers or car sales companies. Some of us will be more trusting of new technologies, enthusiastically embracing innovative products or services. Institutions in which we place varying degrees of trust are the government, police, healthcare, military, church, schools, media, justice, labor unions, and many others. For the purposes of this book, we focus mainly on the trust that we have of other people, also known as social or interpersonal trust, but we also discuss trust in political institutions towards the end of this chapter.

An economy can be described as a series of transactions. When we go to the restaurant or visit a doctor, a transaction takes place: we pay in exchange for a product (food, medicine) or a service (being served at our table, receiving a medical consultation). We pay taxes and expect public services in return. Banks making loans and companies investing in projects are both examples of transactions. Without transactions taking place, an economy could not function properly. Virtually every transaction requires some level of trust. When we go to the restaurant, we trust that the food presented to us will be the one described on the menu and of a genuine quality that reflects the price we pay for it. The restaurant trusts us to be able (and willing) to pay for the bill when it is presented to us.

We trust that the value of money we use in our daily lives will be upheld. A bank that grants a loan trusts its client to repay it. A mining company investing in a new project trusts its engineers and financiers in providing accurate recommendations as to the viability of the project.

In modern societies, trust alone is not sufficient. We do not blindly trust a doctor in giving us good medicine or a restaurant in serving tasty and healthy food. Governments do not just trust their citizens in paying their taxes. Banks do not grant loans solely on the basis of their trust towards their clients. There are various ways to complement trust when entering into transactions. The most obvious is a functioning legal and regulatory framework. If we do not pay our taxes or repay our bank loans on time, we can expect to incur penalties. Pharmaceutical products go through a rigorous process before they can be commercialized, and doctors are required to have specific qualifications before they are allowed to practice. Another way to complement trust is to gather as much information as possible. Consulting reviews of a restaurant, hotel, or airline increases the likelihood that we will not be disappointed with our experience. Before a loan can be provided, banks conduct extensive background checks to assess the creditworthiness of the applicant. Corporate investments are similarly subject to extensive due diligence. In societies where legal recourse is unavailable, threats and retaliatory measures can be an effective, albeit controversial, way of ensuring that each party performs its part of the transaction.

The various measures that complement trust, as necessary as they may be, can be costly. A legal framework involves numerous procedures, lengthy documentation, and potentially expensive legal fees to ensure compliance by all parties. Trust reduces the costs of making a transaction. It improves the efficiency of an economy in which millions of transactions take place every single day. The advantages are not just purely economic: higher social trust has been linked to lower criminality and improved happiness.[3]

Measuring Social Trust

Imagine that you are asked to participate in a game in which you are paired with someone you have never met before. Both of you are given

$100. You are then asked to decide what amount, if any, you wish to give to the other person, knowing that the amount will be tripled. The other person is then asked to make a similar decision: how much money to give back to you, knowing that the amount will also be tripled. How much would you give?

If we were rational people acting purely out of self-interest, we would give nothing. If we give something and the other person keeps the money received without giving any of it back, we lose out. Yet experiments show a very different result: most people do give money and receive some back, making both participants richer. We give money because we hold on to the expectation that the other person will reciprocate. In other words, we *trust* the other person to behave in the same way as we do.

This simple experiment was devised by Joyce Berg and her colleagues in 1995.[4] Since then, several variants have been tested. If the two participants know each other, they are more likely to exchange more money between themselves, a rather obvious result given that the better we know others, the more likely we are to trust them (unless we have good reasons not to!). The more highly educated participants are, the more money they will exchange, implying that those with a higher education have more trust in others. Age and income also increase the amount of money exchanged. But if participants are of a different nationality or a different race, they will exchange less money. In one experiment, where participants were of a different race, 11 times out of 12, no money was given at all.[5] We are less trusting of people who are perceived to be different from us.

When it comes to countrywide data and cross-border comparisons, surveys are required. The most reliable cross-border survey on social trust is conducted by the World Values Survey, which asks the following question: "Would you say that most people can generally be trusted?" Various regional surveys also provide insights into levels of social trust in specific regions.[6] There are several issues associated with surveys that we should be aware of. People may not answer truthfully or may not be aware of their own willingness to trust others. Survey questions may be interpreted in different ways: who exactly are 'most people'? Even if we clarify that these are people we do not personally know, does it refer to fellow citizens, foreigners, or both? In many countries, fellow citizens will be trusted much more than foreigners. Questions in cross-country surveys often need to be translated into a local language, which could lead to mis-understandings. Finally, as is the case with all national surveys, the num-ber of respondents should be high enough in order to constitute a representative sample of the overall population. Despite these shortcom-ings, experimental data and surveys on social trust tend to yield similar results at a country level.[7]

The highest levels of social trust can be found in Nordic countries, where a majority of the population generally trusts others. The top five countries in the world with the highest levels of social trust are Norway, Sweden, Finland, Denmark, and Iceland. Scandinavians feel a sense of togetherness, a belief that solutions that benefit one member of society are likely to benefit all of society. The collective is seen as superior to the individual. Companies are organized in flat structures and the advice of more junior team members is often sought. Decision-making is consen-sual, which delays the process but ensures wide adoption of the decisions made. About two-thirds of Swedes generally trust others, a much higher proportion than any of the other 60 countries included in the World Values Surveys.[8] Not only is social trust high, it is also very stable: in the six edi-tions of the World Values Survey since 1981, social trust among Swedes has oscillated between 52 and 64 percent. The European Social Survey finds similar results, with all Scandinavian countries scoring much better in social trust than other European nations.[9]

Nations of Protestant heritage also display higher social trust than Catholic ones. 40 to 50 percent of the population in the Netherlands, Germany, Australia, New Zealand, and Canada generally trust others, whereas historically Catholic countries such as France, Spain, Portugal, Italy, and Greece trust others much less. Within each historically Protestant country, Protestants have more social trust than Catholics. In Germany, Protestants were found to be almost twice more trusting than Catholics.[10] Similar results were found in the Netherlands and Canada.[11] In the US, however, there is little difference in social trust between Protestant and Catholic communities.[12]

In Asia, China is the country with the highest levels of social trust: about half of those surveyed said that they generally trust others. Yet it appears that many Chinese respondents believe that 'most people' refer to those they already know, such as family members, friends, and other acquaintances, as opposed to complete strangers. When the question is rephrased as 'Do you trust people you meet for the first time?', only 11 percent answered positively.[13] There is no such gap for Nordic and other historically Protestant countries: general levels of trust in others and trust in people whom they meet for the first time are roughly the same. This would imply that social trust in China is not as high as what the World Values Survey implies. Another Asian country with high social trust is Thailand, perhaps a result of Buddhist traditions that emphasize tolerance towards others.

At the other end of the spectrum, citizens of the Middle East, Africa, and Latin America are far less likely to trust others. Ongoing conflicts in the Middle East and some parts of Africa, as well as the legacy of the slave trade in many African countries, have done little to make people trust each other more. Latin American countries have some of the worst levels of trust anywhere in the world: only 5 to 15 percent of the population trusts others in Brazil, Argentina, Colombia, Chile, and Peru. 82 percent of Brazilians believe that most people seek to gain advantage over others regardless of ethical considerations.[14]

The Origins of Social Trust

Why are some societies almost devoid of social trust whereas others have a majority of people who generally trust each other? Various explanations into the origins of social trust have been put forth: the less hierarchical nature of Protestant societies, the long-distance trade networks of the Vikings, a tradition of voluntary association, the establishment of functioning institutions, rising inequalities, high levels of crime, or the legacy of the slave trade. We will never know for sure the true origins of social trust in each society, but they would appear to date back decades or even centuries ago. We learn to trust or distrust people as we grow up. Once we have been taught whether others can be trusted, we tend to stick to that belief throughout our lives and transmit it to the next generation.

This idea that social trust constitutes a value transmitted from one generation to another is evidenced by the fact that social trust is remarkably stable over time. Year after year, the number of people who trust each other within a specific country or community remains roughly the same, even when comparing data decades apart.[15] Even countries which have experienced dramatic economic changes in their modern history have retained roughly the same levels of trust in others. The inter-generational transmission of social trust is further evidenced with data from the US. Since 1972, the General Social Survey has been asking Americans whether they trust other people and recording the ethnicity of those taking part in those surveys. Every year, the most trusting Americans are those of Nordic descent, which are, on average, 35 percent more trusting than the rest of the population. Their level of trust matches the one found in the country of their ancestors: Americans of Swedish descent trust others in the same proportion as the citizens of Sweden.[16] They have been established in the US for generations, are governed by the same institutions, and are subject to the same policies as their fellow citizens; and yet they are much more trusting of others than their fellow citizens. US citizens of Italian or Spanish descent show much less trust in others, in line with levels of social trust found in Italy or Spain.

That is not to say that social trust can never change over time. At the individual level, someone who trusts others may lose that trust as a result of a traumatic event or a series of negative experiences. In 1948, in one of the earliest examples of surveys on social trust, nine percent of Germans trusted others.[17] That generation had gone through years of war and deprivation, preceded by a period of hyperinflation that destroyed the value of their savings. They had understandably lost trust in the world around them. Throughout the 20th century, as the war generation made way to a new one that enjoyed an economic revival, social trust in Germany gradually increased to 45 percent.[18] A US study has found that one of the main factors leading people to trust others less is a traumatic experience such as a divorce, disease, accident, or financial misfortune.[19] But in the absence of such life-changing events, social trust remains stable over time.

Social Trust, Growth, and Inequality

Studies find a strong link between social trust and economic growth.[20] Countries in which people trust each other, and are therefore able to transact more efficiently, are on average more likely to reach higher levels of development. This is also true within countries: in the US, states with higher social trust are more prosperous than states where people have less trust for each other.[21] We should not conclude from these observations that economies where people do not trust each other can never grow. Brazilians have little trust for others and yet have seen their economy grow strongly in the second half of the 20th century, and again during the first decade of the 21st century. But a lack of social trust makes it more difficult to attain higher economic growth given the additional costs incurred.

Another common feature of societies where people generally trust others is that they tend to be more equal. Nordic countries, where social trust is the highest in the world, also have the lowest levels of income inequality. Latin American countries, where people are the most distrustful of others, are among the most unequal. Although social trust has remained stable in most countries, it has declined in the US and the United Kingdom (UK). In the US, social trust declined from 46 percent of people who generally trusted others in 1972 to 32 percent in 2016, a 30 percent drop. The United Kingdom has seen a similar trend. That period also coincided with a significant increase in inequalities in both countries, both in terms of income and wealth.[22] This has led to the idea that rising inequalities have reduced social trust (more on that below).

Could a more unequal society make people less trusting of others? The logic behind this argument is that we are closer to those who share the same economic background as us. In a highly unequal society, if those at the bottom perceive society as unfair, if they feel discriminated against or even exploited, they will have little trust for those at the top. If this holds true, the solution is straightforward: reduce inequalities by raising taxes and redistributions, and social trust will increase again.

There is probably some truth to the idea that inequalities can reduce social trust. But this theory rests on the assumption that social trust is solely the result of our life experiences. It ignores the fact that social trust, to a large extent, is the result of the values we inherit as we grow up. As we have seen, social trust has remained stable over time for most countries. In Germany, for example, income inequalities have gone up since the 1980s but social trust has not declined. It seems more plausible that instead of inequalities resulting in lower social trust, it is higher social trust that results in lower inequalities. People will be more accepting of wealth redistribution through higher taxes and government expenditures when trust is high. However, this does not mean that a country with high social trust will automatically proceed with more redistributions. But at least it has the option to do so (and probably should).

The Impact of Migration on Social Trust

We have left one question unanswered from the previous section: why did social trust decline in the US and the UK, both by around 30 percent, whereas in other countries it has remained mostly stable? Numerous explanations have been provided, such as lower participation in voluntary associations, higher inequalities, higher television viewing which reduces the level of interaction that people have with each other, the rise of consumerism, and the decline in civic involvement. But other industrialized countries have experienced similar factors and yet did not witness a significant decline in social trust.

We see two reasons why social trust declined in the US and the UK, and they both relate to migration. First, the arrival of migrants who originate from places where people generally do not trust each other into a society with higher levels of social trust will inevitably, at least initially, reduce social trust within that society. Consider a group of people. If we were to add new members to the group, with less trust in others than existing members, the overall level of social trust of the enlarged group would automatically decline. This has nothing to do with any interaction between group members: at this stage, the existing members continue to trust others the same way as they did before the arrival of new members. Lower trust in others is simply the result of how the composition of the group has evolved.

Since the 1960s and 1970s, the US has seen an influx of Hispanic and Black migrants from countries where social trust has been historically low. Hispanics now make up 18 percent of the US population, up from just 4 percent in 1970. Most Hispanics in the US come from Mexico, a country where only a tenth of the population generally trust others. Blacks now represent 13 percent, up from 11 percent in 1970, and also mostly originate from low-trust countries. In the UK, social trust dropped by more than 30 percent within less than a decade, from 44 percent of people who generally trusted others in 1990 to just 30 percent by 1999. The 1990s was a decade of immigration in the UK as more than 100,000 net migrants entered the UK each year, a significant change from previous decades.[23]

If we assess the decline of social trust in the US and the UK by observing the ethnic composition of their population and measuring levels of social trust in the countries where migrants originated from, we find that social trust would have decreased between 10 and 15 percent from 1970 to 2016.[24] So the decline in social trust can be partly explained by the evolution of the ethnic composition of US and UK populations, but not entirely. This leads us to the second reason why social trust has declined in these two countries: the impact of migration on the local population's existing levels of social trust.

Let us return to our example of people with low social trust joining a group where existing members have more trust in others. What happens then? We have seen that cultural distance makes a difference: if migrants are well-educated, speak the local language, or share the same ethnicity and religion, their interactions with the group will be made easier and they integrate faster into their new society. Social trust levels of the existing group members remain unaffected. But if those who join the group do not speak the local language, if they live among themselves, or if they commit crimes, they will not be trusted. In order to trust someone, that person needs to be trustworthy. If that is not the case, the trust that people have for others will inevitably decrease. Existing members of the group will feel that the newcomers cannot be trusted and will not open up to them; newcomers will feel discriminated against and their own level of social trust, which was already low to start with, may decline even further.

In both the US and the UK, the large number of migrants entering the country has led to populations becoming less trusting of others. Although the topic is hotly debated, there is evidence that higher net migration has led to lower social trust, with the integration of migrants depending, to a large extent, on cultural distance.[25] In the US, neighborhoods with more racial mix have seen lower levels of trust.[26] We are not arguing here for migration to developed countries to be curtailed; there are many reasons, economic and humanitarian, why migration should be pursued. Over time, migrants are expected to contribute positively to economies affected by ageing populations and a shortage of low-skilled labor. But it all boils down to whether they can blend into their new environment; failure to do so would result in a loss of trust, potentially leading to lower growth and higher inequalities.

We should also point out that a homogeneous society is no guarantee that its people will trust each other: Russia and Sicily are very homogeneous yet there is little trust among their people. But social trust does tend to decline the more ethnically diverse a society becomes.

Migration and Trust in Sweden

From 2008, Sweden welcomed large numbers of migrants, with more than 100,000 settling in every year. By 2016, in the midst of the European migrant crisis, a record 163,000 entered the country and a total of more than 1 million new migrants became part of a population of just 10 million over a decade. Sweden has welcomed more migrants than any other European country relative to the size of its population. The country is relatively large, but migrants tend to settle in and around the biggest cities: one third of all residents of Malmö, the third largest city in Sweden, were born outside the country. Populations in certain districts of Stockholm have up to 40 percent of non-Swedish natives. Almost one in four living in Sweden is born outside the country, a much higher proportion compared to other Nordic countries.[27]

Sweden has a long history of welcoming migrants. In the 1960s and 1970s, they were predominantly from Italy, Greece, and other Scandinavian and Baltic countries, as well as Iran during the Islamic Revolution. The 1990s saw a surge of refugees from the Balkans. In the 2000s, Iraqis were the ones fleeing war. Successive waves of migration created anxiety among the Swedish population as some worried that those from very different backgrounds might not be able to adapt to Swedish society. In the 1970s, one prominent diplomat stated, "He or she came from a country or a culture whose customs and practice are so alien that a somewhat harmonious adaptation is difficult or impossible."[28] In the end, not everyone adapted to Swedish society, but most people did. The overall impact to the economy has been overwhelmingly positive, with migrants increasing the workforce of a rapidly ageing society. Many of them did jobs that locals avoided in sectors such as healthcare, agriculture, or catering. Levels of trust remained high throughout those years.

Will things be different this time? The number of migrants is much higher compared to what it used to be: the 163,000 migrants who arrived in Sweden in 2016 is twice as high compared to those who arrived in 1992 at the height of the war in the Balkans. People also come from further afield, from the Middle East and Africa, places where the cultural distance with Sweden is higher. Many have few job qualifications and do not speak English, let alone Swedish. Less than 5 percent of jobs in Sweden are considered low-skilled, compared to 9 percent in Germany and 16 percent in Spain.[29] This makes it difficult to find a job: only half of all migrants managed to secure one.[30] Some migrants feel discriminated against when applying for jobs, complaining that with equal qualifications, Swedish candidates are given priority. Studies have shown that ethnic discrimination does play a role in the Swedish labor market.[31] But not everyone is actively looking for a job: it is easier to rely on generous state benefits than to toil in low-paid jobs. Others will only accept jobs under certain conditions, for example, insisting that the job be located in the same neighborhood as the one they live in.[32]

Some Swedish citizens are losing faith in the system. As they finance generous benefits enjoyed by an increasing number of people who do not pay taxes and who struggle to adapt to their new environment, those citizens question whether they are being fairly treated. As they watch gangs made up of mostly migrant youth burning cars and throwing stones at police and firefighters during successive riots that started in Malmö in 2008, they began to question whether people really can be trusted. There is evidence that social trust is being eroded. A study comparing Swedish regions with low and high levels of past migration between 1998 and 2013 found that in those regions with a high proportion of migrants, social trust has declined, whereas it remained stable in regions with lower migration.[33] Those who have lived in Sweden for generations have become less trusting of others as a result of recent migration. The study also found that migration from other Nordic countries (the Finnish represent the largest group of foreigners in Sweden) had no impact on social trust. This is not surprising given that people in Scandinavian countries share similar values.

The country probably welcomed too many migrants in 2015 and 2016, threatening its welfare system by weakening social trust among the Swedish population. In light of growing discontent over its immigration policy, Sweden tightened its rules. Fewer migrants were allowed in the country: 2017 marked the first year since 2012 that the number of migrants arriving dropped below 150,000 people. Certain benefits given to migrants were scrapped. These changes were necessary to avoid an even deeper drop in social trust among the population. Recovering trust will take time. It takes time for migrants to learn a new language and acquire the skills required to find a job. One hopes that over time, they will be able to settle in, adapt to Swedish society, and contribute positively to the economy, as did previous generations of migrants before them.

Political Trust

Do you trust your government?

If you are a citizen of Northern Europe, even more so if you are Scandinavian, your answer is likely to be 'yes'. Elsewhere, trust in government is low and declining, unsurprisingly so when so many politicians seem to end up in corruption probes, extramarital affairs, or other unflattering situations. The same international divide that exists for social trust extends to trust in governments: people who trust others, on average, also trust their governments. But contrary to social trust, political trust is volatile. In democracies, we are more trusting of leaders whom we voted for and far less trusting of those we voted against. The state of the economy is another important factor: when times are bad, the government often gets the blame. Major events caused by external forces that unite a nation increase trust in governments, sometimes spectacularly so, as it did in the US after the September 11 terrorist attacks.

The long-term decline of political trust in many western societies is often seen as a grave threat to the stability and legitimacy of political institutions in those countries. These threats have yet to materialize as governments continue to operate despite weaker political trust. In most democratic regimes, voters may have little trust for politicians, but they remain deeply attached to democratic principles. In some cases, we should also distinguish between various levels of government: in China, the central government is generally considered to be more trustworthy than provincial, prefectural, or county governments.

Another implication for political trust is the redistributive function of the state. If the government is to manage the wealth of its citizens through taxes and state expenditures, there has to be an element of trust between citizens and their government. If not, this opens the door to various forms of abuse. For the state to play a significant redistributive role and tackle growing inequalities, social and political trust are a prerequisite. The relation between social trust, political trust, corruption, and fiscal policy will be further discussed in subsequent chapters.

Chapter 4

Risk-Taking

Eric stormed out of the room, clearly unhappy with the way his meeting had unfolded. He was attending the bank's credit committee meeting to advocate for a credit line to one of his new clients, a local producer of heavy machinery. The committee declined to pursue the opportunity further. The credit manager vetoed it, justifying his decision by the company's relatively small size and an uncertain industry outlook despite strong financials and a potentially high return for the bank.

Eric had spent weeks preparing his application and trying to convince his employer to proceed with a credit facility. This was only the latest example in a long list of rejected new clients. He even struggled to renew loans for his existing clients and began to wonder how he was supposed to contribute to the bank's bottom line if virtually all his applications were turned down. He was particularly incensed at his colleagues from the credit department who had the authority to decline any new application. They had little incentive to approve a transaction that had a remote possibility of incurring losses and seemed oblivious to the expected returns, only focusing on potential losses. The only files that seemed to receive their seal of approval were the largest, most creditworthy clients of the bank, companies that showed little interest in obtaining further funding from Eric's bank and generated low returns as they had many other options to secure new financings.

For the past 20 years, Eric had worked as a relationship manager at PrudentBank, a regional bank specializing in loans to businesses. The last decade felt very different from the previous one. When Eric started his career, the only thing that really mattered were the profits he generated. But in this new world, a typical day involves preparing reports that few people ever bother to read and arguing with his credit and compliance departments. He understood the purpose and relevance of those departments, but felt that things had gone too far. He was now spending more time on internal administrative matters than managing and trying to grow his portfolio of clients.

The mood at PrudentBank had become gloomier over the years. With most applications to the credit committee either turned down or significantly curtailed, revenues and margins had declined. Rather than trying to improve revenues, the bank focused on costs instead. Employees were let go, sometimes replaced by others in distant, lower-cost countries. Wages, bonuses, and other entitlements had all been reduced. Gone were the days of high year-end bonuses and fancy bank events. Even taking a client out for lunch or accepting small gifts now required a full internal report. Eric had to squeeze into economy class seats on most of his business trips; he found himself traveling much less as a result.

Some of Eric's colleagues had enough and left the bank. Others were eagerly waiting for their retirement or desperately looking to switch industries. Eric was also contemplating his options, but he knew that other banks had adopted a similar approach; the grass did not seem any greener elsewhere. As staff morale declined, revenues continued to drop. Management responded with further rounds of cost cutting. Eric wondered where it would all end.

He knew that this trend was not entirely the bank's fault, which had to comply with much more stringent regulations. The entire banking industry had been affected. Eric's managers would also point to weaker economic prospects to justify the bank's actions. Yet Eric felt that the banking industry was at least partially responsible for those weak prospects: if banks no longer supported businesses, how were those businesses supposed to grow? PrudentBank's management were proud of their conservative approach, yet an overly conservative approach had contributed to much lower profits. Returns and risks go hand in hand. Companies that hope to enter into low-risk and high-return transactions will struggle to find many such opportunities. PrudentBank is a reflection of the profound changes that many banks have gone through over the past few years, sitting on large piles of cash and struggling with lower margins, failing to fully perform their role as financial intermediaries because of an unwillingness, and sometimes an inability, to take risks.

Risk-taking

Risks are everywhere. We may not always realize it, but each day we are faced with numerous risks, some of them more likely than others and some of them more consequential than others. We risk arriving late for work if we wake up later than expected, the car we drive could be caught up in an accident, the food we consume may cause us health issues, and so on. We can reduce the likelihood of some of these risks from occurring by purchasing a reliable alarm clock, driving carefully, subscribing to an insurance policy, or eating healthier food; but there are other risks, such as falling victim to a terror attack, that can be more difficult and sometimes impossible to avoid.

Some risks are easier to evaluate than others. The likelihood of losing money in a lottery or being involved in a car accident are examples of measurable risks. But the risk that an economy will suffer a deep recession within the next two years or that there will be heavy rain in the coming week are much more difficult to quantify. The Covid-19 pandemic is one such example of a risk that could not have been realistically forecasted. Because we often use mental shortcuts in an attempt to simplify the complex reality that surrounds us, we may struggle to assess risks accurately, even measurable ones; our perception of the risks we face does not always reflect reality.

Most of us are risk-averse: given the choice between a certain outcome and an uncertain one, even if the uncertain outcome provides us with a slightly higher *average* return, we still proceed with the less risky option. We tend to avoid uncertainty and act accordingly. Some of these decisions will be trivial, but others can have life-changing consequences: pursuing studies in a promising but untested field, accepting an overseas posting, running a business venture, or starting a family. The same applies to the corporate world: to grow further, businesses regularly invest in projects that inevitably entail some form of risk. These projects can turn out to be very profitable or, in the worst of cases, precipitate a company's downfall.

Risk is often portrayed in a negative light. People tend to associate it with gambling or speculation. Excessive risk-taking can certainly lead to potentially disastrous consequences. But if we tried to eliminate all risks, we would struggle to progress. If people never change jobs, never start a new business, never drive or fly, never put at least some of their savings into more risky assets, or if businesses never venture into new projects, economies would stall. Risk-taking forms an inherent part of our societies. Risks need to be identified, understood, and managed (to the extent possible), but they should not be completely eliminated.

Measuring Risk-Taking

One way to assess how individuals deal with risk is by putting them in hypothetical situations where they are asked to make a risk-based decision. If you are given the choice between being awarded $5,000 or flipping a coin where you can either earn $10,000 or nothing, what would you do? Most people will choose the safest option and take $5,000. We also fear losses much more than we value gains. If we are given a choice between *losing* $5,000 or flipping a coin where we can either *lose* $10,000 or break even, most of us will choose to flip the coin to have a better chance of avoiding a loss.

Experiments that involve risk-taking have their limitations. People may act very differently during an experiment compared to a real-life situation. Whether the payoffs are real or hypothetical plays a role: we tend to take the experiment more seriously if we can earn real cash. Our behavior also changes if we are playing for $2 or $20,000.[1] Another way to measure risk preferences is to look at aggregate data that involves risk-taking, such as the use of seatbelts whilst driving or subscribing to insurance policies. The assumption here is that these are reliable proxies for the general risk-taking behavior of individuals. But an entrepreneur who has taken calculated risks throughout her life could well be wearing a seatbelt whenever she drives. The United States (US) is one of the largest insurance markets in the world per capita, but this does not mean that Americans are highly risk-averse individuals.

The difficulty in finding a suitable proxy for risk-taking means that when it comes to cross-country comparisons, surveys are the preferred tool. The World Values Survey asks participants in more than 50 countries about their attitude towards risk-taking. Those with the highest tolerance for risk can be found in Africa: only 9 percent of Nigerians, 10 percent of South Africans, and 15 percent of Ghanaians consider themselves risk-averse. The corresponding figures are 26 percent for South Koreans, 34 percent for Indians, 39 percent for Americans, 50 percent for Chinese, and 56 percent for both Germans and Brazilians. The country with the fewest risk-takers? Japan, where 66 percent of respondents are reluctant to take risks.[2]

Another survey that measures risk preferences is the Global Preference Survey, which collects data from 80,000 people in 76 countries, representing about 90 percent of the world population. The results are quite similar to those of the World Values Survey: African nations show a higher appetite for risk-taking, whilst Japan is again among the most risk-averse. The US, United Kingdom (UK), and Sweden are also more willing to take risks than the likes of Germany, France, or Brazil.[3]

Do people in poor countries, on average, have a higher propensity to take risks? The logic here is that the more we have (in terms of wealth and income), the more risk-averse we become because we have assets to protect, whereas if we have very little, we do not have much to lose, giving us a higher incentive to take risks. Yet the data shows otherwise, at least at a country level. Yemen and Haiti are impoverished nations, yet according to the World Values Survey, 60 percent of their population are risk-averse. At the other end, Singapore and South Korea are highly developed nations but only a quarter of their population would consider themselves as risk-averse. No significant relation exists when comparing risk preferences for the 56 countries that took part in the latest World Values Survey with each country's gross domestic product (GDP) per capita.[4]

Horror Movies

Although we take more risky decisions in certain aspects of our lives and more conservative ones in others, on average some of us will be more risk-averse than others. This could be due to a multitude of factors: age, marital status, wealth, income, or the sector we work in, to name a few. We often take fewer risks as we become older, if we are married, or if we have a stable and rewarding job.

A major reason why risk preferences evolve over time has to do with economic prospects, or rather, *perceived* economic prospects. In one experiment, participants were asked to watch a clip from a horror movie with their risk preferences assessed shortly after viewing the clip. They would be asked questions such as whether they wished to invest in risky assets. Other participants were asked to answer the same questions without having watched the horror clip. Those who watched the clip were on average less inclined to take risky decisions than those who did not (unless they enjoy horror movies, in which case watching the clip had no impact on their risk profile).[5] If we are personally affected by an event, especially a traumatic one, we tend to become disproportionally risk-averse. The effect is usually temporary; over time, risk preferences revert back to what they were prior to the event. But in some cases, a countrywide shock can have a long-lasting impact on the risk preferences of a population with dramatic consequences to the economy.

Risk attitudes fluctuate through economic cycles. When an economy is booming, people and businesses will become more eager to take risks, less concerned about the possibility that things may go wrong. During the dot-com bubble at the end of the 1990s and again during the mid-2000s, there was a belief among many that stock and housing prices could only go up. But when a recession hits, we become much more conservative. Part of it is rational: if we are at risk of losing our job or expect a lower future income, we spend less. Businesses that forecast weaker demand for their products or services will be less inclined to invest in new projects. But part of it is more emotional. As a crisis hits, businesses may decide to stop new projects completely, even those that make economic sense. Households may start saving a much higher portion of their income, more so than what rational expectations would dictate. During the 2008 crisis, risk aversion reached historical highs in the US and many other countries: investments dried up, banks would not lend to each other or to businesses, and households reduced their spending to minimal levels. Office workers would even make fewer trips to the dry cleaner, saving a few dollars each week.

Risk preferences do not only manifest themselves over economic cycles and future economic prospects. If that were the case, South Koreans would not be twice more willing to take risks than Germans. Haitians would not be six times less willing to take risks than Nigerians. Risk aversion is also a value that people grow up with. It does fluctuate depending on economic conditions, but it tends to fluctuate around a specific level that is unique to each country and reflects the aggregate attitude towards risk of an entire population.

Similar to hard work, thrift, and trust, when we observe the risk preferences of migrants, we find that these preferences correlate with those in their country of origin, unaffected by their new socio-economic environment. In the US, a study that looked at the country of origin of chief executive officers found that those who originate from countries with a lower risk tolerance are less committed to acquisitions and capital expenditures, even in cases where their family have been in the US for decades.[6] Whilst first-generation migrants retain the risk preferences of their country of origin, the evidence from several studies is less clear when it comes to second or third generations of migrants.[7] Risk aversion is a value that is probably less 'sticky' than other values explored in this book when it comes to intergenerational transfer.

Religion and ethnicity also seem to play a role in shaping risk attitudes. There is strong evidence that the more religious a person is, the less willing that person is to take risks (at least in western societies, maybe less so in Asia). Atheists exhibit a much higher willingness to take risks than Christians or Muslims.[8] In terms of ethnicity, Blacks and Hispanics in the US tend to be more risk-averse than Whites, even compared to lower-income Whites, possibly due to larger family sizes.[9]

Why Is There No Silicon Valley in Europe?

Attitudes towards risk can have long-lasting effects on innovation, a major driver of economic growth. Many studies show a negative correlation between risk aversion and entrepreneurship.[10] The reason is simple: people who are willing to take risks will be more inclined to start a business. Nations where more people are willing to take risks such as South Korea, the US, or Japan before 1990 have historically been much more innovative than the rest of the world. Among second-generation migrants in America, risk preferences in their country of origin has a significant impact on the likelihood of them becoming entrepreneurs: an Indian migrant in the US will be more likely to start his own venture than a German migrant.[11] In Europe, people are on average less willing to take risks and start a new business, which reduces their ability to innovate. The old continent has many prestigious universities and research is heavily subsidized, yet this seldom translates into innovative products or services. China has made considerable progress, providing funding and state-of-the-art facilities to its researchers, but still has a long way to go before it can be considered as an innovative nation. At a time when technological change is becoming ever more disruptive, innovation is likely to play an even greater role in the economic destiny of nations. Whether a nation is an innovative one depends on many factors, among which include an educated workforce, a supportive government, available funding, and a strong legal framework. But even with all these factors in place, a country will struggle to innovate if its people are unwilling to take risks, fearing potentials losses more than they value potential gains. This has been the case with Japan for the past three decades.

Risk Aversion in Japan

Most of the issues that plague the Japanese economy can be attributed to the extreme risk aversion of its citizens since 1990 when the country experienced a deep financial crisis that it never truly recovered from. Risk aversion has permeated the entire Japanese society. Japanese households are reluctant to spend their disposable income, fearful of an uncertain future, opting instead to deposit their savings in bank accounts or purchasing government bonds, none of which provides any meaningful return. Banks find themselves sitting on piles of cash, unsure of what to do with it. Second or third-tier banks are the most affected as they often focus exclusively on the domestic market. Investment as a part of GDP has gradually fallen since 1990.[12] As of mid-2019, Japanese companies were holding on to almost five trillion US dollars of cash and cash equivalents.[13] The fear of failure associated with projects means that Japanese companies prefer to sit on their cash reserves rather than enter into new ventures.

The lifetime employment system that still prevails in many companies is not conducive to risk-taking: employees are carefully monitored, given few responsibilities, and rarely rewarded for their personal achievements.

In a country with the highest life expectancy in the world and a declining population, adequate returns need to be generated from pension funds to ensure there will be sufficient funding available to retirees. Yet the country's public pension fund, the largest in the world with more than US$1 trillion of funds under management, earns a paltry 1.5 percent return each year, far lower than what a well-diversified portfolio would be expected to generate.[14] Here again, risk aversion is the culprit. The managers of Japan's public pension fund are so conservative that they invest more than half of the available funds into domestic bonds that generate no returns. A well-diversified global fund yielding a 5 percent average annual return would have returned at least an extra US$350 billion over a decade.

Risk-averse Japanese citizens have become increasingly wary and unfamiliar with what is happening outside their borders. At a time when more students around the world study overseas, gaining valuable international experience, Japanese students stay at home: those studying abroad fell by 36 percent between 2004 and 2014.[15] Common reasons include the fear of living in a very different place, the language barrier, and the belief that it would jeopardize their chances of finding a good job at home. But it is precisely this overseas experience that would help them improve their level of English, an asset that Japanese companies should value more highly. Despite weak growth prospects at home, Japanese companies are increasingly making products and services for their domestic market only. This tendency for Japan to turn its back to the outside world is sometimes referred to as the Galapagos Syndrome, named after Sharp's Galapagos tablet that launched in 2010 and only catered to Japanese consumers. Other products that were successful in Japan but never quite made it overseas include NTT DoCoMo's i-mode in 1999 that enabled users to view websites on a phone, a 'wallet mobile' launched in 2004 in partnership with Sony for payments to be made by swiping a phone onto a card reader, and a technology introduced in 2006 that displayed television programs on mobile phones or personal computers. These were all groundbreaking products that could have captivated a global audience. But the fear of venturing outside national borders has resulted in significant global market share losses. In a familiar pattern, Japan would develop the right technology but too often allow international competitors to become world industry leaders.

Even the ability to innovate has waned over the years. Very few Japanese aspire to become entrepreneurs. Most graduates end up joining large corporations. A study by a consultancy found that only US$800 million of venture capital had been provided to Japanese firms in 2015, compared to US$8 billion for India, US$49 billion for China, and US$72 billion for the US.[16] The World Bank ranks Japan 89th for the ease of starting a business behind Afghanistan and Burkina Faso.[17] According to a survey, only one quarter of Japanese view entrepreneurship as a good career choice and less than four percent have the intention of starting a business in the next three years, ranking last out of a sample of 52 countries.[18] Japan is clearly not (or no longer) a nation of entrepreneurs. When Prime Minister Shinzo Abe visited Silicon Valley in 2015, he bemoaned the lack of a risk-taking culture in Japan, stating, "This is something that is most needed by Japanese businesspeople."[19]

It would be unfair to lay all the blame for the dearth of entrepreneurship solely on a lack of risk-taking. Japanese entrepreneurs face more risks and challenges and enjoy fewer rewards compared to entrepreneurs in other developed nations. Banks are unwilling to get involved, and even if they were, they would insist on a personal guarantee. Limited liability is a fuzzy concept in Japan: in the event of a bankruptcy, the entrepreneur will often remain personally liable, a responsibility that sometimes extends to his immediate family. Public funding for research and development is available, but only to large firms. In the late 1990s, many venture capital agreements had a clause stating that if the company did not complete an initial public offering within two years, its promoters could be forced to repurchase all shares from investors at a pre-agreed price.[20]

Even if funding can be secured, newly-formed companies struggle to attract employees and commercial partners. Few workers will contemplate joining a new venture. Suppliers and customers will be reluctant to get involved, preferring long-term relations with established counterparts. In *Japan Restored*, economist Clyde Prestowitz describes the struggles of Kyocera, a ceramics and electronics manufacturer founded in 1959, which first had to make its name in the US market before it grew to a size that entitled it to deal with Japanese counterparts.[21] Even successful ventures provide little upside to local entrepreneurs when their firms go public as public offerings of start-ups generate only limited interest from domestic capital markets.

Individuals are not the only ones shying away from innovation. Japanese companies, once a beacon of technological advancement around the world, and despite their access to significant research and development funding, have failed to roll out truly innovative products in the past 30 years. In 1945, Sony started as a small repair shop with a handful of employees in Tokyo and went on to become one of the most innovative companies of the 20th century. Such a feat is unlikely to be repeated. Research on groundbreaking products will often not be pursued as the risk that consumers fail to adopt them will be considered too high. Instead, the products that come out of Japanese factories tend to be marginally superior to existing ones. The country continues to rely heavily on fax machines and physical stamp seals. A former deputy head of cybersecurity admitted to never having used a computer in his entire professional life.

None of the various policies over the past 25 years aimed at lifting wages or prices, and ultimately spurring growth, has produced significant change. The reason is that 'nudging' consumers and companies to change their behavior is not enough. It is not enough because risk aversion, like other human values, is firmly embedded in people's minds. People seldom change their values, except in life-changing circumstances such as the crisis of 1990 that was traumatic to many Japanese and severely altered their attitude towards risk. The only way to achieve meaningful results for the Japanese economy is through drastic action: by forcing change onto people and businesses. Wages can only go up meaningfully if companies are forced to apply wage hikes. A radical but effective solution would be to force companies to increase wages by a certain rate each year, say two or three percent, for *both* public and private companies, as long as those companies remain profitable. Each year the government would assess the situation and decide on an appropriate wage rate increase. This would come at a cost to employers. But the expectation is that with workers earning more, they would also spend more, ultimately stimulating growth for the country. It is unclear what portion of their higher wages they would be willing to spend, but they should be inclined to at least spend *some* of it. Other areas where drastic action could be taken include forcing public pension funds to allow for a much higher allocation to risky assets, including non-Japanese ones; forcing most university students to spend at least one semester abroad; clearly removing any personal liability that comes with starting a new business; forcing banks to allocate a minimal portion of all loans granted to small and medium size companies, as well as better report and manage their bad debts; and removing regulations that prevent fair competition, such as the protection enjoyed by convenience stores in the retail industry.

Secular Stagnation

We argued in previous chapters that a traumatic experience such as a war or a deep recession has the power to change, at least temporarily, the values that people associate with. This is also true of risk aversion, as we have seen in the case of Japan. There are fears among some observers that the same fate awaits the rest of the developed world following the 2009 financial crisis and now the coronavirus pandemic. Anemic growth over the past decade has revived the notion of *secular stagnation*, the idea that countries may be experiencing a permanent or at least a prolonged period of low growth and low inflation. Secular stagnation was first articulated in 1938 by economist Alvin Hansen at a time when the US had experienced almost a decade of subdued growth.

If the developed world is indeed engulfed in a state of secular stagnation, why is that so? There has been no shortage of explanations. One is demographics, the idea that, as populations age and the working-age population shrinks, GDP will inevitably follow the same trend. Another is the rise of inequalities. Low-income and middle-class households spend a higher portion of their revenues compared to those with higher income levels because basic costs such as housing or food represent a higher portion of their income. Faced with stagnating or even declining wages, those households are unable to increase their level of spending, a major driver of growth in most countries.

The issue with the idea that demographics or inequalities is responsible for a prolonged period of slow growth is that those are not new phenomena. The financial crisis did not cause populations to age or inequalities to widen. Developed economies were already faced with those challenges long before the 2009 crisis hit. In fact, lower birth rates and an aging US population (together with slowing innovation) were factors pointed out by Alvin Hansen to justify anemic growth in the late 1930s. He would be proven wrong as the US embarked on a military spending spree and enjoyed decades of prosperity after World War II.

Yet another justification for secular stagnation is the decline in real interest rates, that is, long-term rates less the prevailing inflation rate. Real interest rates are negative in many developed countries as long-term nominal rates have fallen to record lows, close to zero or even entering negative territory. The belief here is that central banks are unable to drive *real* interest rates low enough to incentivize people to spend and businesses to invest. The only way out, as argued by proponents of this theory, is for economies to engage in fiscal stimulus, namely government spending.

As we have noted in the chapter on thrift, long-term interest rates are low not so much because of investor expectations, but because of global imbalances in savings rates, with excess savings in some parts of the world making their way into countries where savings are lower than investments. It appears very unlikely that consumers would decide to permanently reduce their consumption and businesses to permanently reduce their levels of investment simply because interest rates are not low enough, despite them already being at historically low levels. It takes time for economies to recover from crises as severe as the Great Recession of 2007–2009 and similarly in regards to the Covid-19 pandemic. As the memory of the crisis fades away, as a new generation of people enter the workforce without having personally experienced the crisis, economies will continue to go through their cycles of booms and busts. Growth and inflation were similarly subdued in the decade that followed the Great Depression of the 1930s. Investors from that era mostly kept away from equities throughout their lives. Those who experienced high inflation rates in the 1970s would continue to expect higher prices decades later, scarred for life by events that occurred earlier in their lives.[22] Every time a developed economy shows signs of slowing down, the specter of secular stagnation is revived and slow growth is expected to become a permanent feature. The strong growth that the US experienced from 2015 to 2018 is evidence that its economy is not stuck in a state of permanently low growth. With the notable exception of Japan, talks of secular stagnation are likely to eventually fade away as people and businesses regain their confidence.

Financial Intermediation at Risk

There is, however, one aspect holding back the ability of consumers to spend and businesses to invest: the extremely high risk aversion of the banking sector. Banks have become much more risk-averse since the financial crisis in terms of their lending practices. Many businesses, especially small and medium-sized enterprises (SMEs), are unable to expand their operations or even finance their working capital needs as they struggle to obtain the necessary funding from banks. This is important because SMEs constitute the lifeblood of most economies, contributing greatly to employment, job creation, innovation, investment, and overall economic activity.

US companies are less affected by the reluctance of banks to make loans available to them because many of them are able to tap into developed capital markets for their funding requirements, whether debt or equity. In China, privately-owned companies have long struggled to access financing, but this is entirely policy-driven, unrelated to risk preferences by local banks. But in Europe, where SMEs rely almost exclusively on banks to finance their operations and contribute 85 percent of new jobs, 58 percent of GDP, and 67 percent of employment, they are struggling to access cash.[23] In the UK, whilst the number of SMEs has grown by four percent annually from 2013 to 2017, the number of loans and overdrafts approved has decreased by seven percent annually over the same period.[24] In the eurozone, whilst German and Dutch SMEs are still relatively well supported by their banks, SMEs in southern European countries (Italy, Spain, and Greece) are facing higher rejection rates and more expensive terms. By one estimate, SMEs in the European Union are thought to be lacking 400 billion euros of bank financing.[25] Bank costs for European SMEs have increased disproportionately compared to large firms since the financial crisis, a worrying trend that the Covid-19 pandemic will have exacerbated.[26] More banks have been lending to SMEs during the pandemic, but only because those loans were guaranteed by governments, often in full, making them essentially risk-free.

European economies are hampered by other factors as well, from aging populations to sclerotic and overregulated labor markets. But by acting in such a risk-averse manner, banks are not fulfilling their main function, which is to act as financial intermediaries by channeling cash between depositors and borrowers. Most banks nowadays are highly solvent and liquid, yet are very restrictive with their lending practices, especially towards less creditworthy counterparts.

It would be unfair to lay all the blame on banks for their highly conservative approach. Only a decade ago, they were accused of taking reckless risks (although a more accurate description is that they did not understand the risks they were taking). A few years later, they are being accused of not taking *enough* risks. Banks have to comply with much stricter regulations, forcing them to allocate a larger portion of capital to more risky loans that reduce their incentive to chase higher risks despite higher potential returns. Losses are to be avoided at all costs, even when those losses are dwarfed by much higher expected gains. Risk departments have become key decision-makers and have little incentive to approve new lending (and potentially expose themselves to criticism when a loan they approved turns sour). Many European banks are also struggling with an oversized network of physical branches; some have been slow in investing and adapting to new technologies. The consequence is lower revenues and lower margins. The return on equity (ROE), a common proxy for profitability, for eurozone banks has languished at levels of three to five percent in the years that followed the financial crisis. In more recent years, but before Covid-19, returns have climbed to five or six percent, but remain much lower compared to US banks that generate ROEs of 10 to 12 percent.[27] The low profitability of eurozone banks is not a result of negative interest rates. Clearly negative rates are not helping the banks, but if they significantly affected returns, Nordic banks, which were among the first to operate in an environment of negative rates, would not be generating returns on equity of around 10 percent.[28] Eurozone banks have responded to lower revenues by cutting costs. Virtually every European bank has gone through extensive cost cutting programs in the past years. 75,000 jobs cuts were announced in 2019 in the banking industry, the majority of them in Europe.[29] Once the obvious choice for most graduates of business schools, banks have now become much less attractive potential employers.

The solution when it comes to funding industries, and particularly SMEs, may come from alternative sources of financing. One option is securitization, in which SME loans are pooled together in a structure that repackages these loans into a tradable security. Some banks are actively involved in these structures, which allows them to sell some of their SME exposure to other investors. Another option is peer-to-peer lending, where financial technology (fintech) companies provide a common platform to SMEs and potential investors with standardized rules and documentation. Some of these platforms have received approval by national regulators, improving their legitimacy. Credit guarantees provided by insurers and various other parties can also assist companies in accessing financing. Lastly, funds and other shadow bankers are playing an increasingly large role in financing businesses, filling the void left by banks. These entities are more lightly regulated and willing to take higher levels of risk in exchange for higher returns.

Different Countries, Different Outcomes

The remedy commonly advocated by economists to escape secular stagnation, more public spending, may help, but it does not address the root cause of the problem. Japan's successive rounds of fiscal stimulus have not had much impact on its economy. We should recognize the role played by risk preferences over the willingness of households to consume, businesses to invest, and banks to lend, and realize that within the developed world, we are faced with three very different cases. Risk aversion in Japan has played, and will likely continue to play, an outsized role in preventing its economy from growing significantly again. In the US, risk aversion plays a much smaller role in shaping long-term economic trends; its economy will continue to go through cycles of faster and slower growth. Just as they did after the 1930s, talks of secular stagnation in the US would eventually become outdated. In Europe as well, risk aversion is unlikely to have permanent effects on households and businesses.

However, and especially in continental Europe, banks have become very risk-averse and slow to adapt to a changing world. Striking the right balance between taking on too much or too little risk is not easy, but even still, bank lending has become overly conservative in the past decade. European businesses have historically relied almost exclusively on banks for their financing, doing little to diversify their sources of funding. This will have to change.

PART II
POLICIES

Chapter 5

Political Stability

December 2015 marked the proclamation of the Republic of Logone by Muslim rebels as a response to the ongoing civil war between Christians and Muslims in the Central African Republic, a small, landlocked country located, as the name implies, in the center of Africa. Two years earlier, a group of Muslim rebels had seized the capital Bangui with their leader declaring himself president. He remained in power for less than a year. Both communities have been accused of committing atrocities, with more than a million people believed to have fled their homes in a country of less than five million.

This was only the latest episode in a long list of coups and civil wars since the country gained independence in 1959. The first coup in 1965 was made by Jean-Bédel Bokassa, a larger-than-life character who would rule the country with an iron fist for 14 years. The husband of 17 wives and father of a reported 50 children, he converted to Islam at one point but had a change of heart three months later, converting back to Catholicism. He devised a rather creative way of reducing unemployment, forcing every citizen of working age to prove they had a job or risk being fined or imprisoned. Bokassa kept good relations with former colonizer France, taking President Valérie Giscard d'Estaing to hunting trips and offering him diamonds, ultimately causing a scandal in France and contributing to Giscard d'Estaing losing his re-election. Self-declared Emperor of Central

Africa, Bokassa was ruthless with anyone who disagreed with him. He was rumored to have killed one of his political opponents by "carving him with a knife that he had previously used for stirring his coffee" and, so the story goes, was particularly fond of human flesh, keeping butchered bodies in a cold-storage room in his palace. Human flesh was allegedly served to Bokassa and his guests on several occasions, including during the visit of foreign dignitaries. Bon appétit...

He was eventually overthrown and put on trial for ordering the murder of up to 100 children and personally participating in the executions, "smashing their skulls with his ebony walking stick", after some of them had the impertinence of throwing rocks at his Rolls-Royce, unhappy about being forced to purchase and wear school uniforms imposed by Bokassa. Towards the end of his life, he proclaimed himself the 13th Apostle and claimed to have secret meetings with the pope.[1]

After Bokassa, the country remained mired in violence. In 1993, its first freely elected leader, Ange-Félix Patassé, hailed from the northern tribes, the first president to do so. As he appointed mostly fellow tribesmen to key government positions, members of the southern tribes became infuriated, reducing his legitimacy. Patassé never had the full support of the army, which was dominated by officers from southern tribes and was eventually toppled in 2003 in yet another coup. A civil war ensued between government forces and various rebel groups, including the Muslim minority representing about 10 percent of the population. Ceasefire and peace agreements were subsequently signed, but violence continued and the armed conflict resumed in 2012. Although a democratically elected leader has been in place since 2016, infighting has persisted to this day, mostly between Christian and Muslim communities.

Throughout its history of violence, the Central African Republic has remained among the poorest nations on Earth, with political instability preventing any form of economic progress.

Debunking a Myth

For decades, it was a common belief in the West that democracy was *the* path to long-term prosperity. Rich countries were virtually all democracies whereas most poor countries had far less democratic regimes in place.

Examples abound of despots enriching themselves at the expense of their population, in the most severe of cases leading to famines, armed conflicts, and mass unemployment. The logical conclusion was that democratic institutions, free press, and freedom of speech without fear of persecution were key drivers of growth. This vision of the world also fit nicely with the values espoused by most in the western world. Loan packages to poorer countries were often (and, in many cases, still are) conditional to the emergence of democratic institutions, a key component of the so-called Washington Consensus that originated in the United States in the 1990s and provided a list of recommendations that was seen at the time as a magic formula that would lead every nation on a path to sustained development.

A few rebellious countries had other ideas. Park Chung-hee of South Korea and Augusto Pinochet of Chile showed little interest for democratic principles, yet their countries managed strong economic growth during their dictatorships. Other countries embraced democracy but saw little economic impact. India had become the world's biggest democracy upon independence in 1947 but suffered a dismal rate of growth until much-needed reforms were enacted in the early 1990s. Ghana's economy fared no better in the first decade since becoming a democracy in 1992. Yet democracy enthusiasts were undeterred. India, Ghana, South Korea, and Chile were seen as mere outliers, poor or small countries that were nothing more than an afterthought in the wider global economy.

The first cracks in the narrative that democracy was a precondition for sustainable growth appeared in the 1990s with studies finding little relation, or even a negative one, between democracy and growth.[2] Not everyone agreed, with other studies coming to the opposite conclusion.[3] Even if such a link existed, did democracy lead to higher growth through institutions that create a system of checks and balances, or did growth lead to democracy as populations become more highly educated and urbanized, aspiring to higher political freedom? And how exactly should democracy be measured? A country may officially be a democracy but lack democratic institutions. This all created a heated and seemingly endless debate.

And then China came along. Its autocratic regime was never an impediment to its spectacular growth; in fact, many in China firmly believe that the absence of an electoral process has made its institutions stronger, whereas it promotes constant bickering, short-termism, overspending, and unfulfilled electoral promises in democracies. Several western commentators have predicted, and some continue to predict, the inevitable fall of China if the country does not proceed with democratic reforms. It is a common fallacy among forecasters to cling onto their predictions despite clear evidence that those predictions have long been disproved. China's success has led to countries around the world questioning the wisdom of a democratic transition as they grow their economies.

The objective of this chapter is not to argue in favor of one form of government or the other. But when it comes to economic growth, our contention is that the type of government does not matter much. What really matters is political stability.

Political Instability and Growth

Political *instability* is never a good thing. It creates confusion, inefficiencies, and wastage. The worst manifestation of political instability is war. In a war, lives are lost, infrastructure is destroyed, and funds are diverted towards war efforts as opposed to more productive uses. Countries engulfed in conflicts often struggle with vast amounts of money flowing out as foreign investors repatriate their funds and citizens transfer their wealth abroad. The intellectual elites flee the country, sometimes permanently. The consequences can be devastating, with populations displaced, savings wiped out, and entire industries that grind to a halt. Poor countries are the main victims of political instability, but rich countries are not immune to it, although in their case things seldom escalate into full-blown conflicts. Belgium was without a government for 18 months in 2010–2011; Australia had six different prime ministers in nine years from 2010 to 2018; Japan, not to be undone, had seven prime ministers in seven years from 2006 to 2012. These situations are certainly not conducive to higher growth but at the same time, have not been detrimental to it; if anything, it is evidence of the limited impact of politics on economic life.

Political stability reduces the uncertainty that companies and households are faced with, leading to a better allocation of resources. However, this is not always true: North Korea is politically stable, but its economic performance has been disastrous during most of its modern history. Eritrea, a small nation at the eastern tip of Africa, is another example of a politically stable country with very limited growth. Clearly, there are other factors at play when it comes to economic growth that will be explored in subsequent chapters. But overall, political *stability* is more conducive to economic growth than political *instability*. The International Monetary Fund reviewed 169 countries between 1960 and 2004, using cabinet changes as a proxy for political instability, and concluded that political instability is associated with lower growth. Other studies have come to similar conclusions.[4] As is often the case with those studies, the causality is unclear: higher stability should lead to higher growth, but higher growth should also make citizens more contented, giving them less of an incentive to unseat their government. What is likely at work is a virtuous cycle whereby stability leads to higher growth which itself leads to higher stability.

The Conflict Trap

If a virtuous cycle exists in some countries, others are stuck in a vicious one, characterized by endless conflicts. Conflicts predominantly occur in very poor countries, but not always: Algeria, Egypt, and Thailand are examples of middle-income nations where governments have been toppled in the past decade.

The term 'conflict trap' was first coined in 2002 by economists Paul Collier and Nicholas Sambanis to describe countries mired in conflicts.[5] A country with a recent history of violence is more likely to fall into another conflict in the future because a culture of violence has taken place. The number of homicides *after* a conflict has ended is often higher compared to the period preceding the conflict.[6] Even soccer players are impacted. In 2011, Edward Miguel and his colleagues from the University of California looked at the country of origin of all players in the top five soccer leagues in Europe to determine whether those players had experienced civil war. They then compared that data to the number of yellow cards received by those players, with the idea that the majority of yellow cards handed by referees relate to violent conduct on the pitch (red cards as well, but since there are relatively few of those distributed during a game, yellow cards provide a better sample). The authors found that players from conflict-affected nations had received a disproportionally high number of yellow cards, leading to the conclusion that violence remains ingrained in people even years after leaving their home nation. Players from Colombia and Israel, the two countries that had experienced civil war every year since 1980, received the most yellow cards.[7]

Military expenditures typically remain high even after a conflict has ended, diverting funds from sectors such as education and healthcare. Countries stuck in a conflict trap struggle to extract themselves out of it and remain very poor. Collier advocates the use of foreign military intervention to stabilize a country in the first few years after a conflict has ended, something that developed countries have shied away from given that committing resources, especially human lives, to faraway conflicts is seldom a popular choice back home.

A democratic transition could help poor countries escape a conflict. Unhappy citizens in a democracy always have the option to vote their elected leaders out at the next election, an option that would be unavailable in an autocracy. But the reality is that newly-established democracies in very poor countries remain fragile and exposed to the risk of being either dismantled in a coup or abused by unscrupulous leaders.

Ethnic Diversity

Whilst historical battles were often motivated by territorial claims, most modern conflicts find their roots in ethnic or religious considerations. It has become unusual nowadays for countries to go to war with one another; conflicts are mostly within countries, whether they take the form of civil wars, coups, or mass demonstrations.

Whether ethnic diversity increases the likelihood of conflicts remains a matter of academic dispute.[8] But in ethnically diverse countries, it does seem likely that autocratic regimes struggle more than democratic ones to generate growth. This is because the autocratic leader, in most cases originating from the majority ethnic group, will often defend the interests of that group at the expense of minorities. In the words of Paul Collier, "Diversity tends to narrow the support base of the autocrat. [...] The narrower the base of social support, the stronger the incentive for economic policy to sacrifice growth in order to redistribute income to the autocrat's group."[9] There are indeed many examples of ethnically diverse autocratic countries where the ethnic majority manages the economy in favor of itself with little consideration for other ethnic groups. This often results in lower growth and instability: there comes a point when the exploited minority will seek to change things, whether by leaving the country, calling for independence, or fighting against the established regime. The persecution of Shia and Kurdish minorities in Iraq under Saddam Hussein, the plight of the Rohingyas in Myanmar, and the genocide of the Tutsi minority in Rwanda are all examples of conflicts where autocratic leaders have favored their own group at the expense of others. This line of reasoning also explains why China, which has a relatively homogeneous population, has prospered without democratic institutions; or why India, a country with a much more diverse population, would probably struggle without a democracy because the interests of its minorities would be less represented at the national level.

Even if minorities have little chance of being in power, their interests tend to be better represented in a democracy. Ethnically diverse societies are less prone to conflicts if they are run as democracies. We should not necessarily conclude from these observations that societies which are both ethnically diverse and autocratic cannot prosper. If the autocratic leader does not seek to favor his or her own ethnic group at the expense of others, the autocratic regime in itself should not be an impediment to growth. As long as the leadership of an ethnically-diverse country does not put minorities at a disadvantage, it should make little difference whether the government is a democratic or autocratic one. Even modern democracies tend to discriminate against minorities, usually in more subtle ways.

Political Stability and Social Trust

Another reason for political instability is a lack of social trust. In societies where citizens trust each other, they are less likely to resort to violence against one another as a way of expressing their discontent. More decisions will be made by consensus, with a genuine attempt to find the best solutions for everyone. Countries with higher social trust (Nordic nations, Northern Europe, Canada, Australia, and New Zealand) have been among the most stable politically. Although the elected party or leader can change frequently, as is in Australia, differences between the main political parties are relatively small. It is rare for people to hit the streets, and when they do, protests seldom turn violent.

One could argue that these are all prosperous countries; people should be less inclined to challenge the status quo. But even when economic conditions deteriorate sharply, things do not escalate as they do in other countries. In the early 1990s, Sweden's economy went into a severe recession and unemployment rose above eight percent. At around the same time, Canada suffered a recession in which 11 percent of the active population was unemployed. Yet Swedes and Canadians, whilst understandably frustrated by this turn of event, did not engage in mass street protests or try to topple their government. Citizens of countries with high social trust are, on average, less inclined to take drastic measures, keenly aware that violent action would ultimately be detrimental to their society.

Countries with low social trust, even developed ones, are more prone to violent action. France, where social trust is relatively low, has a history of violent action against political leaders, most recently with the yellow vest protests. The Arab Spring uprisings took place in countries where people have little trust for one another. Latin America, the region with some of the lowest levels of social trust in the world, has had its fair share of military coups and abrupt changes in government policy. So have many African nations. A 2017 study that compared measures of social trust and political stability across more than 50 countries from 1950 to 2008 concluded that poor economic performance is more likely to cause political turnover in countries with low social trust.[10]

Leadership

Sometimes all that is required to stabilize a country is an exceptional leader, whether democratically elected or not. Deng Xiaoping, Nelson Mandela, Mahatma Gandhi, Seretse Khama, and Lee Kwan Yew are all examples of leaders who have earned great legitimacy (and their rightful place in history) by transforming their respective countries. None of them favored their own ethnic or tribal group, instead ensuring that the voices of other groups were heard and acted upon.

There are many reasons why a country may be politically unstable: economic mismanagement, rising inequalities, a history of conflict, an incompetent leader who clings on to power, ethnic diversity, or low social trust. Even geography plays a role: a population spread around a large and difficult-to-reach territory makes it easier for rebel groups to develop and hide. Out of all these factors, low economic growth is usually at the top of the list of factors leading to instability. However, this is not always the case: the economy was not the main priority of the likes of Mandela and Gandhi, who had higher aspirations for their people and faced more pressing matters. But over time, as people's basic needs of finding a job and earning a decent living to feed themselves and their families take center stage, only a strong economy can fulfill these needs, and a prerequisite to a strong economy is free markets.

Chapter 6

Free Markets

1982 was not a good year for Chile. The national soccer team had lost their three games at the World Cup in Spain over the summer. But to Chileans back home, even soccer-obsessed ones, that was the least of their worries. Their economy seemed decimated. Gross domestic product (GDP) had plunged a massive 15 percent. A quarter of the working-age population was unemployed, with those out of a job receiving little support from their government. Banks had become insolvent. Foreign investors were exiting the country in droves. Local producers were unable to compete with cheaper imports. Half of the population fell below the poverty line, earning less than a dollar a day. Angry and destitute citizens took to the streets.[1]

The crisis, the deepest that was to hit Chile in living memory, was a shock to many, not only in the country but also outside of it. The United States (US) and the wider international community had been impressed by the way Chile had transformed itself, having devised and implemented bold economic reforms after socialist rule had been abandoned nine years earlier. To global policymakers, economists, and investors, Chile had effectively become a real-life successful example of the recently established economic orthodoxy of unregulated, free markets.

As Augusto Pinochet came to power in 1973 in a bloody military coup, replacing the socialist government of Salvador Allende, Chile suffered from hyperinflation and mass unemployment. In need of urgent and far-reaching economic reforms, Pinochet reached out to a group of Chilean scholars who had studied economics at the University of Chicago. They became known as the 'Chicago Boys' and were put firmly in charge of economic matters. Despite little practical experience, they were convinced that free markets were good for all purposes; that markets 'always knew best'. In their view, private companies should be left to compete with each other and state intervention minimized. According to that line of thought, acquired during their university years but still very much prevalent to various degrees in academic circles to this day, an economy going through a crisis would have to fix itself without any state interference, whatever the financial and human costs involved. As the Chicago Boys went to work, this ideological belief in free markets and absence of state intervention was applied to virtually all sectors of the Chilean economy, including trade with other nations and the role of the state in redistributing wealth. These ideas were implemented in record time: most public companies were privatized, the banking sector deregulated, trade barriers and capital controls removed, taxes and state expenditures lowered significantly, new companies given unrestricted access to markets, and struggling ones forced to shut down. The Chicago Boys were also dogmatically intent on fighting inflation, which plagued most Latin American economies at the time. That meant increasing interest rates to very high levels to break inflation expectations.

These various measures worked well for five years. Between 1977 and 1981, *real* GDP increased by eight percent on average every year. Public deficits turned into surpluses. Inflation was reduced to single digits, one of the lowest in the region. Seduced international investors lent record amounts of money to Chilean banks and industries. By late 1981, however, things started to unravel. A constant push for lower inflation generated massive unemployment. Low taxes and equally low social benefits meant that Chile became the most unequal society in Latin America in a region already known for high inequalities. Lifting trade barriers resulted in foreign products flooding the local market, comprising 25 percent of all sales in the country by 1982. Local producers were simply unable to compete and produce what a growing middle-class wanted to buy: television sets, video recorders, or cars. As for exports, with the exception of copper, Chilean producers had little experience dealing with international markets. As exports languished and imports surged, large trade deficits became the norm.

Since 1979, the local currency, the peso, had been pegged to the US dollar at a rate that was never subsequently revised. Such a policy would not have been advocated by the Chicago Boys and contributed to the crisis by making imports too cheap and exports uncompetitive as the peso soon became overvalued, and also by bringing in too much short-term foreign capital. US investors had been attracted by high interest rates and the fixed exchange rate with the dollar. They could convert their dollars into pesos, earn a high return, and then convert back into dollars at the same exchange rate. They still faced the risk that the companies they were lending to would go bust, but at least the exchange rate risk was neutralized (as long as Chile kept the rate fixed). The country became a magnet for dollars, not so much for long-term productive projects, but for a quick profit. The trade started to look less attractive in the early 1980s as the US Federal Reserve increased its own interest rates in a bid to fight high inflation at home. At the same time, the Chilean banks and companies that foreign investors had lent to were struggling to repay their loans. By now, investors were taking their cash out of the country, a scenario that Thailand and other Asian nations would become all too familiar with 15 years later. Chile struggled in vain to keep its fixed peg. In the end, as its reserves of dollars dried up, the peg had to be abandoned.

Local businesses struggled with excessive levels of debt; the inflow of international money had simply been too large for the Chilean economy to handle. The country would end up with a massive debt where the accumulated interest alone represented 70 percent of the debt outstanding by the end of 1982. Many banks and financial institutions had to be nationalized, a rather unusual outcome for a government that privatized most of the economy just a few years earlier.[2]

Following the 1982 crisis, Pinochet needed a change of direction, appointing Hernán Büchi as finance minister in 1984. Although Büchi did not study in Chicago, he held similar views as the Chicago Boys on free markets. But he was much more pragmatic. Distancing himself from grand theories, he was a practical man who implemented gradual changes to see what worked and what did not. His first priority was to restructure the external debt. A more flexible exchange rate was put in place, frequently devaluating the peso until the currency was allowed to float freely. New banking regulations provided increased transparency and accountability. Since local producers were unable to compete with global competitors in many sectors, tariffs on imported goods were imposed, as high as 35 percent before being gradually reduced in the years that followed as Chile moved from a predominantly agricultural society to an industrialized nation. The government also began to promote exports through tax breaks.

Pinochet's successor in 1990, Patricio Aylwin, focused on reducing poverty and inequalities whilst upholding the principles of free markets domestically. Income taxes were increased and new social programs implemented. Healthcare and education were significantly improved. Short-term foreign investments were taxed to prevent speculative flows into the country and avoid large fluctuations that could destabilize the economy as they did back in 1982. During Aylwin's tenure, the economy grew strongly and inequalities were reduced. The leaders who followed enacted several more reforms, but did not deviate from the basic idea that market forces should be the main engine of growth for the economy.

The results have been impressive. Since 1982, the Chilean economy has been one of the fastest growing in the region. Chile is one of the best-performing economies in Latin America today (its GDP per capita is only surpassed by Uruguay). Inflation and unemployment are both low by international comparison. Its financial sector is stable and modern. Whilst exports are still heavily reliant on copper, the country has become a large exporter of other products, of which fish and wine are perhaps the better-known examples. Despite the spectacular growth of the economy, inequalities have remained at similar levels to those seen in other Latin American nations. At the heart of Chile's success is the realization that, despite necessary regulation, free domestic markets work best.

Domestic Free Trade

Around the world and across centuries, free trade *within a nation's domestic market* has proved to be the best way to create wealth. When prices for goods and services are set by supply and demand, when competition is fair, when barriers for new entrants are low, when insolvent businesses are forced to shut down, or when the rule of law prevails, this all creates an environment where resources are better allocated and innovative ideas foster. Time and time again, countries that have adopted free markets for their domestic economy have seen a surge in growth. The US became the strongest economic power in the world in large part as a result of its highly competitive and efficient domestic market. The western world, as a whole, enjoyed spectacular growth after World War II as state monopolies were dismantled. As a rule, the more countries evolve towards free domestic trade, the higher the economic gains. Across Asia, nations that had previously adopted a planned economy, whether China, India, Vietnam, or Myanmar, have gradually switched to an economy based on market principles, lifting millions out of poverty. Eastern European nations have enjoyed much stronger growth following the fall of the Soviet Union. In Africa, the likes of Angola, Rwanda, or Ethiopia have made relative but noticeable progress after pushing through market reforms.

Nations that have retained their planned economy model, relying on state monopolies and domestic trade restrictions, have been left behind. A lack of competition and implicit state support makes public companies complacent as there is little incentive to innovate or improve productivity. Workers are paid regardless of performance; they have little incentive to work hard or take initiative. The Soviet Union did enjoy fast growth in the 1950s and 1960s but that did not last: growth solely based on the accumulation of capital is not sustainable. Cuba's economy was essentially broke when the Soviet Union collapsed and only recently performed better as it initiated timid market reforms. China and India suffered from dismal rates of growth until they initiated their own reforms. We are not cherry-picking examples: whilst the deregulation of domestic markets has not systematically led to higher growth, there are simply no cases of countries with planned economies that have enjoyed long-term growth.

Creative Destruction

Underpinning the merits of domestic free trade is the concept of creative destruction, a term coined by economist Joseph Schumpeter in 1942. In a society where uncompetitive companies are forced to shut down, this process allows other more competitive and advanced ones to replace them. Examples include the video tape rental industry that was supplanted by the likes of Netflix, traditional libraries that are facing increased competition from online bookstores, or the decline of newspapers at the expense of social media. This ongoing process of destruction and creation enables societies to adapt to technological change whilst ensuring that the surviving firms remain the most competitive ones.

Creating an environment of creative destruction requires certain things to be in place. Clear and enforceable bankruptcy rules are needed to ensure that failing businesses with little hope of recovery are wound down. Companies or individuals that do not abide by the rules of free and fair competition should be held accountable and sanctioned accordingly under a transparent and efficient legal framework. Barriers to entry for new companies, whether explicit or not, should be minimized. New businesses may require funding support in the early stages of their development in the absence of an established venture capital industry. The state should provide a strong educational framework, not only for children and young adults, but also to support workers with lifelong training and re-skilling in order to improve their ability to switch from one industry to another one with better prospects. The state also has a positive role to play in other areas such as setting up technological parks and providing tax breaks to certain key industries.

This all sounds good on paper, yet creative destruction is often met with resistance. Change implies uncertainty, which most of us would rather avoid. The destruction part is clear and often painful: bankruptcies and downsizing inexorably imply that people will lose their jobs. But the number of jobs created is usually less visible and more uncertain. In many countries, governments will come to the rescue of struggling companies, with politicians boasting about the number of jobs they have 'saved' through their actions. In 2013, France's Industry Minister argued that the country had saved 60,000 jobs out of 70,000 that were "threatened to be axed".[3] When Japan introduced a new law in 2009 forcing banks to provide loans to insolvent companies, the Financial Services Minister at the time claimed that his actions had saved "hundreds of thousands of small and medium-sized enterprises".[4]

But are these really the right decisions? What about the jobs that would have been created by having new, more competitive companies replace struggling ones? We do not know whether more jobs would have been created compared to the ones lost. But we do know that by keeping uncompetitive companies afloat, the competitiveness of an entire sector will be affected. Companies that receive support will have fewer incentives to become more efficient because they know the government will be there to support them, whereas companies that did not benefit from state support will feel *unfairly* treated, having to compete against firms that enjoy preferential treatment. Over time, this forms a drag on the economy. Alitalia, the Italian national airline that has almost never made a profit in its 70-year existence, is one company that should be let go: its history is littered with government bailouts and financial restructurings, costing billions of euros to Italian taxpayers. In Japan, as many as 30 percent of companies receive subsidized loans.[5] This has led to the emergence of insolvent, 'zombie' firms. The services sector has been particularly affected: its productivity is only half that of US services companies, barely improving since 1990 and hampered by heavy regulation.[6] A telling example is retail stores found literally everywhere, seemingly at every street corner. Contrary to other countries, they have not been supplanted by department stores or supermarkets. Opening a large store in Japan is an arduous process, one that requires numerous government approvals and can take over a year. This explains why Japan still has more than 50,000 convenience stores scattered across the nation today.[7]

An important aspect of free markets that relates to the notion of fairness described above is that of a level playing field. Companies and individuals have to feel that they operate in an environment where everyone is given the same opportunities to succeed. If that is not the case, if businesses face different tax rates, if not everyone pays their taxes, if land is arbitrarily reclassified, or if corruption is endemic, the system will be deemed unfair and the incentive to perform reduced.

Free markets do not mean that public companies should be excluded from taking part; as long as they are put on an equal footing with their private counterparts and managed efficiently, in a similar way as we would expect private companies to be. Singapore has many thriving public companies that make up a third of all market capitalizations and operate as efficiently as private ones.[8] This model has worked out well, primarily because public companies cannot expect preferential treatment from the government, which does not meddle in their operations. They are subject to the same rules and regulations as private companies.[9] Many of them are listed, further exposing them to market scrutiny and discipline. Public company workers as well as government officials can expect wages similar to those in the private sector. The dominance of large public companies has enabled the country to invest outside its borders, more so than any small or medium-size company ever could, but it has also reduced the ability of local private firms to compete and grow against those much larger players that do not rely on state support but nevertheless benefit from economies of scale. A balance therefore needs to be struck: a competitive market economy cannot be solely comprised of large public companies.

Too often though, state-owned companies are synonymous with bureaucracy, redundancies, corrupt practices, runaway costs, and lifetime employment. A job for life sounds good until we realize that it reduces the incentive for people to work hard and prevents younger workers from accessing the job market. Countries with bloated public sectors almost invariably suffer from excessively high youth unemployment rates.

Limits to Domestic Free Trade

Although free domestic markets are a prerequisite to sustainable growth, it would be wrong to reject all forms of state intervention or regulation on the basis of ideological beliefs, as Chile did in the mid-1970s. There are several limitations to unregulated free markets. First, most markets should not be allowed to develop into monopolies or have a set of competitors agree to maintain artificially high or low prices, with the potential for companies in such positions to abuse their powers by dictating more favorable terms and preventing the entry of other competitors. Exceptions can (and probably should) be made for sectors of strategic national importance such as defense. Second, market practices with the potential to create harm to citizens require added scrutiny. Common examples include false advertisement, healthcare, or the affordability of basic food, in particular when products or services are aimed at the most vulnerable:

children, the elderly, or the less well-educated. Third, certain industries such as public transportation, postal services, water, gas, or electricity providers may have a duty to serve the community in addition to pure commercial motives. This often creates a dilemma, as these two objectives can be in conflict with each other, for example a bus company operating a non-commercially viable route to a remote location where other forms of transportation are limited. Fourth, the rule of law provides an important framework, clearly defining the rights and obligations of each party. This includes intellectual property laws that are required to spur innovation: if anyone can copy the invention of others, there is little incentive for businesses to invest resources into research and development. Fifth, companies facing a temporary liquidity crunch but with otherwise strong long-term prospects may be rescued, more so if they pose a systemic threat to the wider economy, as the banking crisis in 2008 has made abundantly clear. Schumpeter himself favored that view when he stated, "Situations emerge in the process of creative destruction in which many firms may have to perish that nevertheless would be able to live on vigorously and usefully if they could weather a particular storm."[10] But insolvent companies should be let go; rescuing them simply delays the inevitable and hinders the competitiveness of entire industries.

It should be noted here that this chapter is not about fiscal policy. Many free market enthusiasts are ideologically convinced that the role of the state should be minimized in every situation, including when it comes to tax collection and government distributions. We argue in this book that these are completely separate matters. As Nordic countries have clearly demonstrated, high levels of taxation and free domestic markets are not irreconcilable concepts. Nordic countries are sometimes viewed by outsiders as socialist, centrally planned economies in which the government plays a major role in the destiny of local companies. In reality, those economies are market-driven, lightly regulated (except for banks), with few trade barriers, and in which the state only plays a minor role.

International Trade

So far, we have focused on free trade *within a nation*. Yet, companies do not only trade and compete with domestic firms; they do so with international ones as well. International trade, a topic of much dispute recently, had been much less contentious during most of the 20th century. For many years, the consensus was that international trade, just like domestic trade, would bring prosperity to nations that welcome foreign companies, remove trade barriers, and minimize government 'interference'. Many countries have indeed benefited tremendously from global trade, whereas those that have remained closed to the world or have substituted most of their imports for inefficient local production have struggled with anemic growth and outdated technology.

If history is to provide any guidance, a blind faith in international trade is unwarranted. Contrary to popular belief, several nations made significant economic progress during their early stages of development by protecting their industries from foreign competition. The US, for decades the main advocate of unrestricted flows of goods and services across borders, initially limited the ability of foreigners to carry out commercial activities within the country, imposing high import tariffs and actively promoting exports. In 1789, as the young nation was struggling with high levels of debt, Secretary of State Alexander Hamilton instituted a number of reforms that included import tariffs on British manufacturers and subsidies to American industries. At that time, the US was heavily reliant on British imports for its manufactured goods. Import tariffs became the main source of federal revenue and shielded American producers against lower-cost European competitors, paving the way for the rapid industrialization of the country. Tariffs remained in place for more than a century, a period during which the US became the richest nation in the world.

In Asia, the likes of Japan, South Korea, Taiwan, and mainland China all enacted land reforms to industrialize their economy and adopted a series of measures to prevent foreign competition, support their exports, and transfer foreign technologies. During the Meiji Restoration, the Japanese economy opened up to the world but prevented foreign companies from having a local presence. Japanese products at the time were considered inexpensive and of low quality, but the quality soon improved as the country relied on a highly educated workforce and hired hundreds of foreign engineers to learn from western technologies. After World War II, import tariffs remained generally low, but the yen was kept undervalued against major currencies and local market access was restricted through various regulations, including foreign companies' inability to acquire large Japanese entities because of interlocking shareholdings. In South Korea, General Park Chung-hee supported the country's industrialization efforts by providing affordable loans, subsidies, and tax exemptions to its leading export industries: shipbuilding, steel, electronics, and petrochemicals. In China, an undervalued local currency, capital controls, weak intellectual property rights, the availability of cheap funding to large state-owned enterprises, and the obligation for some foreign entities to enter into joint ventures with a local partner are some of the measures that have boosted exports and made it difficult for foreign companies to expand into the country.[11] In all these countries, the idea was to shelter young or 'infant' industries from much stronger outside competition to allow those industries to learn and develop; only once they became more efficient and competitive would they be gradually more exposed to international competition and eventually grow into global players themselves.

Another approach, one that consists of embracing free trade with other nations at an early stage of development, has seen mixed results. Singapore felt it had no choice but to open up to the world upon independence. This has been achieved on an unprecedented scale: the island-state has the highest trade to GDP ratio in the world with imports and exports representing over three times what the country produces.[12] The need to embrace international trade was recognized early on by Lee Kuan Yew. Despite lacking technical and managerial skills, Singapore did not attempt to protect its infant industries. Lee felt confident that its hard-working population, supported by a small but growing group of highly-educated workers and policymakers, would rapidly learn new skills and be able to compete on the international stage, even if that meant being exploited at the beginning: "The prevailing theory then was that multinationals were exploiters of cheap labor and cheap raw materials and would suck a country dry. We had no raw materials for them to exploit. All we had was the labor. Nobody else wanted to exploit the labor. So why not, if they want to exploit our labor? They're welcome to it. And we found that whether or not they exploited us, we were learning how to do a job from them, which we would never have learnt. We were learning on the job and being paid for it."

Singapore has done very well opening its borders after it gained independence, but other nations have suffered detrimental effects in the form of lost jobs, struggling local businesses, and increased reliance on foreign suppliers. One such example is Senegal. The West African country is one of the largest consumers of tomato per inhabitant, with the vegetable found in many local dishes. It is one of the few nations in the region to have a tomato manufacturing industry. When it reduced tariffs on imported tomato paste in 1995 and further in 2000, this led to a surge in imported tomato paste from Europe (which heavily subsidizes its own agriculture). Local producers, mostly small family businesses with limited access to modern machinery, could not compete. Imports of tomato paste have steadily climbed to represent half of the total tomato paste production.[13] Reduced import tariffs have led to lower domestic production and increased hardship for farmers. Ghana, another West African country, has a similar reliance on rice imports, which accounts for two thirds of its national consumption. Despite attempts by the government to increase locally produced rice, domestic farmers are unable to compete with cheaper and better-quality rice from the likes of Thailand and Vietnam.[14] In Senegal and Ghana, local consumers may have benefited from lower prices, but entire industries have suffered.

Even if international trade were to benefit a country as a whole, those benefits can be unevenly distributed among a population. In rich countries, people may benefit from cheaper prices when they purchase goods and services, but that is of little consolation if their wages remain stagnant or if they lost their job to workers in a faraway land who can perform the same task at a fraction of the cost. Finding a new job takes time if the prospects of entire industries are bleak; a steel worker cannot magically reinvent himself as an information technology consultant.

Competing With the World

Why do some economies generally benefit from opening their borders while others do not?

We see two major factors at play. The first one relates to savings rates. As discussed earlier in this book, countries with a higher savings rate, often (but not always) the result of a thrifty population, rely on foreign markets for further growth. Local businesses have to look for consumers abroad if they wish to expand their operations; as such, much of their production will be geared towards exports. This is true of small economies, but applies equally to countries with larger domestic markets. High savings nations such as China, India, South Korea, Japan, Germany, Switzerland, and the Nordic countries all rely on international markets to sell their products and services, and in all likelihood would not have reached their current level of development if they had kept their borders closed. Nations with low savings rates can also benefit from international trade, but those with higher savings rates are much more likely to accumulate excess savings and trade surpluses. Higher savings rates also enable further investment in infrastructure. The import and export of products implies functioning roads, railways, seaports, warehouses, and other logistical assets. Countries that fail to invest in modern infrastructure will struggle to make their exports competitive. On that note, administrative procedures are often overlooked but can seriously derail the efforts of a nation to promote its products to the world: most of the delays in shipping times are due to administrative procedures, whether customs clearance, tax, or cargo inspections.[15] It can take weeks for cargo to cross borders between African countries, causing delays and increasing costs.

The second key factor that determines whether a country will benefit from free global trade is its ability to compete with foreign firms. Emerging countries typically have a cost advantage but lack skills, thereby focusing on products and services with low-added value. Developed countries tend to be more innovative and focus on higher-value products and services, but may not be competitive in terms of costs. Emerging countries will gain from international trade if they have the ability to learn from foreign competitors and acquire their technology. There are countless examples of developing nations that have opened their borders and yet have learnt very little from doing so. Many African states have been extracting natural resources such as oil or minerals for decades but still rely on foreign expertise for those operations. If foreign companies displace local ones, those nations are unlikely to become industrialized.

Local companies need time to acquire knowledge that will eventually improve their competitiveness. Senegal gave foreign firms access to its domestic tomato paste industry too quickly and had to backtrack, re-imposing higher import quotas. The right approach is a gradual and prag-matic one, with incremental changes and regular assessments: if things work well, continue along the same path; if not, reverse course and try something else. The success of this approach and the speed at which it can be implemented depends, to a large extent, on the level of education of the local workforce, which will be the topic of the next chapter. It therefore makes sense for developing countries to protect their industries, at least initially. But that should not become a permanent feature. Excessive pro-tection leads to complacency as local firms, assured in the knowledge that they operate in a protected environment, lack the incentive to learn and improve their efficiency.

As for rich countries that rely on a highly-educated but more expen-sive workforce, overall free trade has greatly benefited them by making it possible for local industries to expand overseas, selling their products and services to a much wider audience and, in some cases, relocating their production, thereby generating economies of scale and ultimately improv-ing their efficiency. The import of cheaper products has also benefited consumers back home. Yet as lower-cost producers, in particular those in East and South Asia, become more competitive, certain companies in the West are no longer able to compete, resulting in the closure of entire industries and the loss of thousands of jobs. The steel industry in the United Kingdom (UK) employed 350,000 workers at its peak in the 1960s. Many towns, especially in the north-east of the country where steel mills were primarily located, relied heavily on that sector. But as Asian competitors started producing and exporting steel at much lower prices, steel mills in the UK could not compete and most went bankrupt. Unemployment in the UK remains much higher in those regions that relied heavily on steelmaking.[16] The process of creative destruction means that the decline of one industry often heralds the rise of another more competitive one. But it can be a challenge for workers to move from one sector to another, especially if their skills are not adapted to those other sectors.

Herein lies one of the main differences between domestic and interna-tional free trade. Within a domestic free and fair competition setting, every company has to follow the same rules. But when it comes to international

trade, the rules are different in each country. Fairness becomes a very relative concept when nations resort to undervalued currencies and forced
technology transfers to gain an advantage. Every country can and should
gain from international trade, but the rules need to be fair, clearly stated,
and respected by all parties involved.

Chapter 7

Education

In November 2001, the OECD (Organisation for Economic Co-operation and Development) Program for International Student Assessment, more commonly known as PISA, published its first international study and country ranking for reading, mathematics, and science literacy, administering tests in the previous 12 to 18 months to more than 250,000 15-year-old students across 32 countries. Although the methodology used to collect data and rank countries has been criticized, on a whole, the PISA studies are viewed as a fair representation of the level of education around the world. As expected, East Asian countries performed well. But the real surprise was Finland, ranked 1st in reading, 4th in mathematics, and 3rd in science. Not only did Finnish students score very highly, they did so across the country, irrespective of the school they attended. This came as a surprise to the Finns: they knew they had good schools, but maybe not *that* good. Some treated the results as a one-off statistical anomaly. But as subsequent PISA rankings were released in 2004 and 2007, Finnish students remained among the best performers.

Prior attempts to compare national education systems never received much media attention. That changed with the PISA studies. Finland's impressive scores, in particular, generated a wave of enthusiasm in western countries. They became curious of a country where all schools are public, classrooms are small, and teachers are given plenty of autonomy.

But what they were most impressed with was the focus on play rather than work: minimal homework, short school days, few tests, and *yet*, those students somehow managed to top world rankings. The fact that Finnish teachers focused their efforts on underperforming students also resonated well with their own vision of what schools should strive to achieve. It seemed like an easy path towards academic excellence, certainly a more attractive one than the East Asian model where, in their view, rote learning is forced on stressed and overworked students.

Government representatives and journalists flocked to Finland to learn about their secret. This 'PISA tourism' would usually take the form of a few leisurely days in Helsinki, visiting a school or two and speaking to teachers and local officials. Visitors would come back excited and convinced that they had uncovered the holy grail of education, recommending a revamp of their own school system to mimic the Finnish model: primary school to start at only seven years old, homework to be scrapped or minimized, a focus on the least performing students, and no examinations. The Finnish system became idealized, with international observers convinced that it could be applied readily anywhere in the world. Some visitors even went a step further, enquiring to the Finnish education minister whether local schools were up for sale.[1]

Holy Grail No More

No work and top grades? It sounded too good to be true. And it was.

Since 2009, Finland's position in PISA rankings has been regressing. In the latest 2018 rankings, the country was no longer in the top 10 in mathematics. It remains well-ranked compared to other western nations, but now lags behind East Asian countries. Singapore, South Korea, Japan, and China have dominated the rankings ever since.

It turned out that the Finnish education system was never quite what foreign observers imagined. They saw the system they wanted to see, failing to realize that the strong performance obtained in the early 2000s was actually the result of a very centralized and accountable system in the 1980s and 1990s, in which teachers had to strictly comply with the assigned curriculum. Those 15-year-old students who took part in the tests in 2000 started school back in the early 1990s. Although reforms had been implemented in the years prior to 2000 to allow teachers greater flexibility, the old system was still very much alive. In 1996, just four years before the first PISA tests, a research team from the United Kingdom was dispatched to Finland to observe the impact of reforms. They saw little change. Reading their conclusion, one could be forgiven for believing that they had just returned from a trip to China and not Finland:

"Whole classes following line by line what is written in the textbook, at a pace determined by the teacher. Rows and rows of children all doing the same thing in the same way whether it be art, mathematics, or geography. We have moved from school to school and seen almost identical lessons, you could have swapped the teachers over and the children would never have noticed the difference. [...] We did not see much evidence of, for example, student-centered learning or independent learning."[2]

Commenting on the PISA results in 2000, a University of Helsinki professor observed that the old system was still the norm: "The model pupil depicted in the strongly future-oriented PISA 2000 study seems to lean heavily on the passed — or at least the passing — world, on the agrarian and pre-industrialized society, on the ethos of obedience and subjection that may be at its strongest in Finland among late modern European societies."[3] In 2005, at a time when Finland topped PISA rankings, 200 Finnish teachers signed a petition lamenting a sharp drop in mathematical ability that prevented many students from reaching a level considered sufficient for university studies in technical and scientific fields.[4]

Results started to decline *because* of the new system that favored play over work. The inconvenient truth is that to achieve high grades, students have to work hard. There are no shortcuts. The focus on equality, whilst commendable, has also had unintended consequences. By following the pace of the slowest children, this slows down the entire classroom, preventing the brightest students from maximizing their potential. Struggling Finnish students used to be transferred into special classes. This changed in the mid-1990s when more and more low-performers were kept in the general system. In 1995, almost all such pupils were taught in special classes, whereas by 2003, 40 percent remained in the general system.[5]

Finland continues to have a strong education system, one of the best in the world. Their focus on equality in the classroom probably contributes to a more equal society. Students who benefit from an approach based on creativity and personal development are arguably better prepared for life as opposed to memorizing and regurgitating abstract concepts. But Finland's academic success was not the result of little homework, few examinations, short school days, equality, public schools, or small classes. It was the result of hard work and good teachers, the two main components of a successful education system.

Innovation, Development, and Growth

"Education is the most powerful weapon which you can use to change the world," Nelson Mandela told his audience in 2003 as he launched a new program aimed at improving education and health levels in South Africa.[6] A poorly educated workforce seriously impedes growth because it prevents workers and companies from becoming more productive and competitive. As economist Amartya Sen put it, a lack of education "is about not having the capability to realize one's full potential as a human being".[7]

Education levels in certain regions are shockingly low. Although significant progress has been made in the past decades, 40 percent of adults in sub-Saharan Africa are unable to properly read or write and many struggle with basic numeracy skills. 9 out of 10 children between the ages of 6 and 14 in the region are not reaching minimum proficiency levels in reading and mathematics. Even excluding children who do not attend school, only two thirds of students enrolled in primary school will be able to complete it.[8] Those students are being robbed of their future. Without proper education, their lives are likely to be a constant struggle. They will contribute little to the growth of their economy; in fact, they are more likely to require support, whether from their family and friends or the government. For children who have experienced armed conflicts, education can provide a brighter future. But without education, too often they remain trapped in a vicious cycle of violence.

In our globalized and increasingly technological world, education is becoming ever more relevant in both rich and poor countries. In more advanced economies, jobs that require few qualifications are being gradually offshored, outsourced, or automated. Some of these jobs, such as taxi drivers, hairdressers, or plumbers, should remain. But as modern societies increasingly focus on high-value products and services, workers who lack the required skills are being left behind. As for emerging countries, developing infant industries and learning from imported technology, both key enablers of growth, can only be done with an educated workforce.

Good education is so important because it is one of the key factors leading to innovation, without which no long-term growth can exist. Innovation is not only about groundbreaking discoveries, it is also about continuous improvements in the way goods and services are produced and delivered. Farms, factories, or offices staffed by skilled workers will be more likely to improve their processes and productivity. The industrialization of nations requires an educated workforce. Machinery and equipment can be imported, but qualified staff are needed to operate those assets. Education may only be one factor contributing to an innovative environment, but without an educated population, efforts to innovate are doomed to fail. Relying solely on outside expertise, as some countries have done, is not a recipe for long-term success.

What Doesn't Work

There is no shortage of solutions offered to provide better education.

One of them is the belief that improving education is a matter of spending more money on education budgets. As it turns out, the amount of money a government spends on education has little impact on the quality of its education system. New Zealand spends more than twice on education than Singapore as a proportion of its gross domestic product (GDP), yet New Zealand ranks 15th in PISA rankings whereas Singapore tops the rankings.[9] The United States (US) spends much more per student than South Korea or Finland but lags behind both countries.[10] More funding therefore makes little difference, at least for richer countries. For nations at an earlier stage of economic development, investing in education does yield positive results because students in those countries desperately need more schools, teachers, and other education staff. According to one study, after spending an initial US$50,000 per pupil throughout their time in school, additional funding brings little improvement, whether in public or private schools.[11]

Another oft-cited solution to improve education is to reduce the number of students per class. The idea is that with smaller classes, teachers can spend more time with each student, helping them improve faster. This is often done in conjunction with more spending: spend more to hire more teachers and increase the number of classes so that the number of students per teacher is reduced. But again, results show otherwise in both developed and emerging countries. China has one of the largest numbers of pupils per class, with an average of 37 students per class in primary school; that figure climbs to 49 in secondary schools, a number that many western teachers would find unmanageable. Yet having so many students per class did not prevent China from becoming one of the best performers in PISA rankings (albeit with disparities between provinces and between urban and rural areas). South Korea, another country that scores very well in PISA rankings, has the second highest number of students per class, 23 in primary school and 30 in secondary school. The country with the lowest students per class was Latvia, with 16 in primary school and 15 in secondary school, yet Latvia was down in 27th position in the 2018 PISA rankings. The US, another poorly-ranked country, had an average class size (public and private institutions combined) of 21 students for primary education and 27 for secondary education.[12] Similar results can be found elsewhere in the world. When additional teachers were hired in Kenya to reduce the number of pupils per teacher by half, there was no noticeable change in examination results.[13]

As we alluded to earlier in this chapter, a strong education is really about two things: hard work and good teachers.

Hard Work

A tourist strolling along the streets of Seoul's affluent Gangnam district in the evening during October or November would be surprised to see a procession of students exiting buildings at 10 p.m. sharp. Those students had not finished watching a movie or ended a video game session. They are enrolled in private tutoring institutes called *hagwon*. Hagwon is big business in South Korea: 13,500 are believed to be located in Seoul alone, often charging high fees for their services. To most Korean parents, this is money well spent in a highly competitive society where college entrance examinations, held every November, determines the future of each student. Things have gotten so much out of control that the government has been forced to impose a 10 p.m. 'study curfew' and authorities routinely raid hagwons to ensure compliance with the curfew. Yet these restrictions are having little effect: hagwons have extended working hours during weekends, given students more homework, or made use of online learning, all with the blessing of parents.[14]

Meanwhile in November 2016, thousands of angry parents hit the streets of Spanish cities to vent their frustration at public schools over the amount of homework forced onto their children. Spanish students are given 6.5 hours of homework a week on average, or slightly less than an hour each day. That is clearly too much for many parents who feel that homework is detrimental to the development of their children. As a sign of protest, they instructed their children not to do any homework over the weekend in an attempt to force the government to scrap homework, so far without success.[15]

The position of Spanish and Korean parents could not be further apart. In *Battle Hymn of the Tiger Mother*, author Amy Chua describes how she educated her two daughters in a 'Chinese way' whilst living in the US. The book caused considerable controversy when it was published, with many in the US accusing her of mistreating her daughters. But when the book was subsequently published in China, many Chinese citizens criticized Chua for not being strict *enough* in the way she educated her children. Whether forcing children to spend long hours doing homework is good or bad for their personal development is debatable. But when it comes to academic performance, hard work makes a difference. In *The World is Flat*, journalist Thomas Friedman quotes a Yale PhD student in biomedical engineering who observes, "So much of science and engineering is about work ethics — the willingness not only to slog through all the fundamentals but also to stick with an experiment even when it fails the first 20 times." Friedman also quotes David Baltimore, the former president of the California Institute of Technology (Caltech), who would "look at the kids who come to Caltech, and they grew up in families that encouraged them to work hard and to put off a little bit of gratification for the future and to understand that they need to hone their skills to play an important role in the world".[16]

In the chapter on hard work, we identified societies that display strong work ethics: East Asian and historically Protestant countries. Nations from those regions dominate PISA rankings. The top 10 countries best ranked in mathematics, science, and reading in the latest 2018 PISA rankings all originate from those regions, except for Poland which ranks 10th in mathematics and Ireland which ranks 8th in reading. Hard-working students achieving better results is no coincidence. It sounds intuitive enough: if we prepare well for an examination, we are more likely to score well. School education in East Asia is often criticized by westerners for its focus on memorization and lack of critical thinking, but rote learning does drill important concepts into the minds of students. Japanese, Chinese, or Koreans do not feel that they were robbed of their childhood for spending so much time studying. Those tuition classes and repetitive work were certainly not fun, but most students, after graduating, are grateful to their parents and teachers for pushing them towards academic excellence as a way to improve their livelihood. Whether we like it or not, our world is a competitive one. Some will get a head start through family and connections, but overall a good education can only improve someone's odds in life. We should, however, be mindful of the fact that stress levels are much higher among Asian students and that this can at times have negative consequences on their well-being.

Just like its Scandinavian neighbors, Finland is traditionally considered as a hard-working society. Similar to *gaman* in Japan and *gemenskap* in Sweden, Finns strongly associate with the concept of *sisu*, a word that describes perseverance in the face of adversity. But in the past 20 years, Finnish students have been given less incentive to work hard. The school material has become easier as it increasingly caters to the least-performing students. Homework has been reduced to just three hours a week. The absence of grades prevents students from knowing how they are progressing. Over time, by putting in less effort, their performance inevitably declines. This is reflected in lower PISA scores.

In 2012, PISA researchers looked at the countries that form part of their survey and how their PISA scores relate to the amount of homework students are given. They found that in most countries, more homework meant better scores. The countries where students are given most homework are all in Asia: Singapore, China, South Korea, and Japan (in some of these countries, students may not have much homework from school, but they spend long hours every week attending tuition classes and receive additional homework from those institutes, or from private tutors at home).[17]

Plenty of homework does not necessarily translate into a good education. American and Spanish students have comparatively more homework than other western countries and yet their PISA rankings are lower. This has more to do with the quality of teaching, as we will see below. Although we cannot prove it, we would venture here that if the quantity of homework in those countries was lower, their PISA rankings would be even lower. There is some evidence that after a certain number of hours of homework, returns are diminishing. At some point, students lose their focus and are no longer as productive. That may be true, but we should not conclude from such an observation that it is useless to study more; the benefits of more hours of homework may be less, but the benefits are still there.

We have argued throughout this book that, barring any traumatic experience, human values are very difficult to change. But with young children still very much in their formative years, values can change more easily. In the US, hard work is at the core of the Knowledge is Power Program, or KIPP, a network of public charter schools (schools that receive state funding but operate independently). Started in 1995 and popularized by Malcolm Gladwell's *Outliers*, KIPP schools enroll students from low-income families through a lottery system (which is mandatory in many US states). More than 25,000 selected students are made to work longer hours each day (9 hours on average), longer days each week (including on selected Saturday mornings), and longer weeks each year (2 to 3 extra weeks compared to other schools). Those who fail to meet work requirements expose themselves to sanctions.

The results have been impressive. KIPP students have consistently outperformed students from other low-income families in other schools, as well as those who had applied to KIPP but did not make it past the lottery system.[18] Some observers feel that people from poor backgrounds are condemned to remain poorly educated, that the odds are stacked against them. It is certainly true that on average, children of rich families perform better at school as they benefit from a more stable environment at home and often have parents who can support them better during their studies. But KIPP schools provide real-life evidence that with hard work, students from low-income households can excel academically and aspire to a brighter future.

Good Teachers

Whilst a focus on hard work has contributed to the success of KIPP schools, that success would not have been possible without good teachers. Hired through a selective process and required to undergo a full year of training, KIPP teachers learn not only about the curriculum they will teach but also about how to manage and lead a classroom. They spend many months shadowing an experienced teacher before they are allowed to teach a class by themselves. They also have to stick to a highly standardized curriculum. As a result of their training, they are better able to earn the respect of their students.

Teachers make a difference. Most of us will remember how some of our teachers inspired us and have had a positive long-lasting impact on our lives. Sometimes it is the opposite: incompetent teachers setting us on the wrong track. Teachers often have a greater impact on us than the school we attend. It starts from a young age: in the US, students who had a more experienced teacher in kindergarten ended up with higher earnings.[19] From a purely economic standpoint, good teachers are those who provide their students with the necessary tools to find a rewarding and stable job as they enter the job market. While hard work as a value depends to a large extent on the society that children grow up in, good teachers are entirely a matter of adequate policies. With the right policies in place, every nation should be able to equip its schools with good teachers. We identify four factors that lead to good teachers: income, status, training, and an incentive to perform.

Teachers have to be paid well, if only to attract top performing students towards a teaching career. That is not to say that aspiring teachers may not view teaching as a noble calling irrespective of how much the job pays, but for most people, compensation is a determining factor in their career choices. Even those aspiring teachers who do not view their future salary as a key consideration may reassess their view a few years down the road as they start to earn a living and pay their bills. Research shows that teacher turnover is higher when pay is lower as low-paid teachers look for better opportunities elsewhere.[20] Higher turnover also means more part-time teachers, leading to a less stable learning environment for students. In Mexico, a study found that higher wages attracted more able teacher applicants as measured by their IQ (intelligence quotient).[21]

Status is also an important consideration for choosing a teaching career path. Some societies respect their teachers better than others. In China, teachers have historically enjoyed a highly respected position. A 2013 study asked respondents in various countries to state, among a given list of professions, which other profession teaching was most similar to. China was the only country that associates teachers mostly with doctors, another highly respected profession. The same study showed that 75 percent of Chinese respondents felt that students respected teachers, by far the highest percentage among the 21 countries surveyed.[22] Within OECD countries, it is in Finland where primary teachers feel the most respected.[23] The Nordic country receives so many applications from aspiring teachers, about 8,000 a year, that it can only accept a tenth of them. All applicants are required to have a university master's degree. Compare this with Greece where half of the population associate teachers with social workers or the US where 40 percent of Americans feel that teachers are mostly like librarians. Teachers do not enjoy a high status in those countries. As a result, the brightest students have little incentive to become teachers: they will search for jobs with higher status and, in many cases, better income.

Teachers' pay and status are often linked, but not always. In Finland and China, teachers do not need to be well-paid to enjoy a high status. But in societies that do not value teachers well, one way to improve their status is to pay them well compared to their peers in other sectors. This can be done by comparing the average teacher earnings to the average earnings of full-time workers in the services sector. In OECD countries, teachers earn 85 percent of the average services sector earnings. Among the least well-paid were US teachers, who earned just 60 percent of average services sector earnings.[24]

Higher pay is not always sufficient to raise the status of teachers. Portugal and Greece are among those countries where teachers earn the most compared to their peers in the services sector, yet they are hardly the most respected. Higher pay does result in a larger and better pool of applicants, thus allowing for a more selective hiring process. But that does not mean that the best candidates get hired. Applicants should be selected purely based on their academic performance. But in countries where corruption is prevalent and teachers enjoy a job for life, the hiring process is far from transparent: those who get hired are often the ones with the best connections or the deepest pockets. This results in the hiring of underqualified teachers, who will struggle to gain legitimacy in the classroom.

Another crucial step is training. Too often it is assumed that a few weeks of training to allow new teachers to become familiar with the curriculum is sufficient for them to start teaching. But having knowledge and being able to disseminate it whilst gaining the respect of the classroom are entirely different matters. It takes months, sometimes years, to become a good teacher. Successful education systems have set up dedicated centers where aspiring teachers spend months understanding the requirements of their job. Finland has 'teacher training schools', affiliated with universities, where student teachers hone their skills as they are monitored by a supervising teacher. Singapore, one of the top-ranked nations in PISA surveys, trains its teachers, recruited among top graduates, for several months at a specialized center. Every teacher is then required to undergo 100 hours of training *each year* to learn about new pedagogical techniques and professional development. Apart from providing teachers with the required tools to succeed in the classroom, teacher schools also standardize the quality of teaching across schools.

Once teachers are adequately trained, they need to be given an incentive to perform. In many countries, teachers are given a job for life and their work is never assessed. This provides little incentive to work diligently or even show up for class. In India, teacher absenteeism is endemic in public schools where it is almost impossible to dismiss teachers and where many of them hold a second job in a private school. In one case, a teacher was absent 23 years out of a 24-year teaching career.[25] In countries such as Peru, Ecuador, Uganda, India, Bangladesh, and Indonesia, on average more than a fifth of primary school teachers were absent during unannounced visits.[26]

Changing such behaviors means giving teachers a better incentive to do their job properly. This involves regular assessment, paying teachers according to their performance, and the possibility of sanctioning and ultimately dismissing teachers who perform poorly. When rural schools in India installed closed-circuit televisions (CCTV) and paid teachers according to class attendance, absenteeism fell by more than 20 percent.[27]

Once structures to protect the jobs of teachers are in place, they are very difficult to change, even if they are ultimately detrimental to students. When Michelle Rhee was appointed chancellor of public schools in Washington, D.C., in 2007, she proposed a two-tiered system where teachers could choose to remain under the existing model of job security and small pay rises, or a new model where teachers would be assessed annually with the possibility to earn as much as 60 percent more but with the risk of losing their job if they did not perform. This was a way of selecting the good teachers (who would join the new model) from the bad ones (who would remain in the old model). However, Rhee's proposal was never adopted by the powerful teachers' unions.

There is one exception to the need to monitor the performance of teachers: countries with high social trust. In those countries, teachers will usually work to the best of their abilities because they see it as a duty to others: students, parents, fellow teachers, and the wider society. They can be trusted to behave in a professional manner. In Nordic countries, regular assessments and wages contingent on performance are not required; in fact, they would be an administrative burden and teachers would feel that their trust is not being repaid. But in countries with little social trust, the performance of teachers has to be regularly assessed for them to be incentivized to perform to the best of their abilities.

Getting Kids to School

For good teachers to provide good education, students first need to show up in class. This is not much of an issue in modern, developed economies where virtually every person goes to school during most of their childhood. But in emerging countries, especially poorest ones, getting children to attend school can be much more of an issue. School may be compulsory, but that does not mean every child actually attends it. Considerable progress has been made in the world in the past decades: the number of students of primary school age not attending school has dropped by 40 percent since 1990, with most of the decline happening in Asia. But there are still 60 million children around the world who do not attend primary school, most of them in sub-Saharan Africa.[28]

The best way to achieve higher school attendance in poorer countries is to make schools free of charge. But canceling school registration fees is only the tip of the iceberg. If parents are still required to pay for school bus fares, uniforms, materials, and lunch meals, they may not be given a sufficient incentive to have their children attend class. From the perspective of low-income parents, a child who attends school represents a cost in terms of school fees and foregone revenue, but also an opportunity for a better, yet unclear and faraway future. A child who stays at home to work in the fields, mines, or factories generates immediate revenue for his family. The tradeoff is a small but sometimes badly needed present income versus an uncertain but potentially larger income in the future. Reducing costs associated with schooling increases the likelihood that parents will have their children attend school. Another option, sanctioning parents who do not send their children to school, especially those guilty of child labor abuse, yields very little result in practice: school attendance does not improve even if parents are sanctioned.

Out of the 53 countries that comprise sub-Saharan Africa, 42 have now made primary education free and most have seen dramatic gains in literacy rates. Burundi abolished school fees in 2005; despite having one of the lowest GDP per capita, literacy rates improved from 54 percent in 2004 to 94 percent in 2010.[29] When students in Kenya were offered their school uniforms instead of having to buy them, school attendance also increased significantly.[30] School enrollment often has a snowball effect: children who see their friends go to school will be more keen to join them. Parents convinced of the benefits of schooling may persuade others to enroll their own children. Countries that experience an initial rise in literacy and school enrollment rates usually see the trend continuing and even accelerating over the years.

School access is another often-underestimated obstacle to getting children to school in poor countries. Haile Gebrselassie is one of the most decorated long-distance runners of all time, winning two Olympic gold medals and four world championships during his illustrious career. He ran with a distinctive posture, his left arm slightly crooked. This was the result of carrying his books under his arm as he ran every morning and every evening the five miles that separated his hometown in rural Ethiopia to his school. Not every child is willing or able to make such sacrifices. Although not every remote area can be covered, countries need to build a sufficient number of schools and provide free transportation so that most children can have access to it. Once a new school is built in a rural area, the challenge is to convince teachers to be stationed there. The best way to entice them is to pay them well, although that may not be sufficient to attract them to more remote locations.

School attendance can also be improved by providing cash to poor parents under the condition that their offspring go to school. Conditional cash transfers, which will be discussed in more detail later in this book, started in Mexico under the PROGRESA program and were so successful that they have spread around the world. Even families that remain unconvinced about the benefits of schooling will be incentivized to send their children to school if they can earn some money in the process.

Of course, this all comes at a cost to governments. But it is worth it as long as the money is well spent. Constant monitoring should be the norm to ensure that education funding is not diverted for other far less productive uses.

Lifelong Learning

When we talk about education, we typically refer to the academic world. That makes sense: most of what we learn tends to be during our studies or the early stages of our career. But once we settle into a job, we usually do not learn as much, believing that the knowledge we acquired early in our lives will be sufficient to carry us through. The problem with this mindset is that the set of skills we acquired during our childhood and early on in our careers may no longer be relevant. Stronger international competition and accelerating technological change increase the probability that our existing set of skills may require some form of upgrade. Growing life expectancy implies more years of working and also increases the likelihood that our knowledge eventually becomes outdated. This is not only a problem affecting rich nations: Chinese or Indian workers with low qualifications are increasingly at risk of having their role automated or relocated to the likes of Vietnam or Bangladesh.

People do not like change. Faced with an uncertain outlook, most of us do not adapt, instead hoping that the uncertain outlook will somehow dissipate. And yet, the world is changing at a faster pace. Governments, in a bid to maximize the *employability* of their citizens, have a duty to identify those industries or positions that are in decline, the ones which are growing (or expected to grow), and how to transfer workers from one to the other. Training programs should be made as attractive as possible: heavily subsidized, offering a wide range of courses, requiring companies to be actively involved in those courses, and regularly assessing their relevance. Unfortunately, workers who are most willing to learn are those who already have high qualifications. The Singapore government, in collaboration with private companies, set up an innovative and heavily subsidized (especially for those above 40 years old) program that offers more than 10,000 training courses for employees to choose from, identifying those skills that are likely to be in high demand in the years to come. Another example is a partnership between Petrobras, the state-owned Brazilian energy company, and Prominp, a coalition of government agencies, private companies, and labor unions, with the aim of identifying shortages in skillsets within five-year plans and training workers accordingly. Prominp has trained more than 100,000 such workers since 2006.[31] More countries should implement similar programs.

Programs should also cater specifically to workers in declining industries. In the Central Appalachian region in the US, the Hiring Our Miners Everyday (HOME) program, launched in 2013, is an effort aimed at helping coal miners affected by the industry downturn. By identifying industries that may require a similar set of skills and providing the necessary re-training and funding, the program has helped almost half of all laid-off workers to find a new job, with many working as electrical linemen. The program also helped with misconceptions, such as that a coal miner has very low skills when in fact many of them operate some of the largest and most complex machines in the world.[32] Now more than ever, governments around the world have a major role to play to ensure that their citizens are equipped with the necessary skills to navigate through an increasingly complex and changing work environment.

Chapter 8

Corruption

On October 14, 1985, Mobutu Sese Seko, the president of the Democratic Republic of the Congo (DRC) for the past 20 years, was celebrating his 55th birthday in his hometown of Gbadolite. To mark the occasion, he had requested the services of Gaston Lenôtre, the lead pastry chef in the world, to fly in from Paris on a Concorde jet to prepare his birthday cake. The main party was held at one of Mobutu's palaces, where guests could enjoy the best dishes brought in from around the world and a wine cellar that was rumored to be one of the finest. Not all the food was imported: the town was surrounded by palm oil, coffee, and coconut plantations; orange and grapefruit groves; and beef and dairy cattle ranches.

Two decades earlier, Gbadolite, located in the northern part of the country next to the border with the Central African Republic, had been a small village composed of mud brick huts. It was literally in the jungle with limited access to bigger cities (Kinshasa, the capital, lies more than 600 miles away). But it also happened to be Mobutu's birthplace. In the late 1970s, he had invested vast sums of public funds to transform Gbadolite into the 'Versailles of the Jungle'. Three palaces were built, complete with paintings, sculptures, and marbled floors; a nuclear bunker, the only one in central Africa, capable of hosting 500 people; a runway long enough to accommodate the chartering of Concorde planes for shopping trips and official visits to Europe; a dual-lane expressway; and a dam at a nearby river to generate electricity. Coca-Cola set up a bottling plant that employed 7,000 workers. Shopping malls, supermarkets, and five-star hotels soon opened. The population rapidly grew to more than 50,000.

Mobutu allegedly misappropriated a total of US$5 billion of public funds during his 32-year reign, much of it transferred to foreign bank accounts and most of it never recovered. His long list of foreign assets included a 16th-century castle in Spain, a 32-room palace in Switzerland, residences in Paris on the French Riviera, as well as in Belgium, Italy, the Ivory Coast, and Portugal. Muhammad Ali and George Foreman were each paid US$5 million of public funds to participate in the 'Rumble in the Jungle' boxing contest in Kinshasa in 1974.

During Mobutu's time in power, the DRC remained one of the poorest countries on the planet. Shortages of food and gasoline were frequent. Runaway inflation made people's savings worthless, whilst Mobutu and his allies held much of their wealth in foreign currency. The excessive money creation that resulted in hyperinflation was, to a large extent, caused by Mobutu treating the central bank as his own personal bank. The country only survived economically through loans from the World Bank and the International Monetary Fund, money that, to a large extent, also ended up in Mobutu's pockets. Those institutions were probably aware that the money was misappropriated, but they kept on lending more, supporting an ally that was seen as fighting communism during the Cold War.[1]

Corruption Takes Various Forms

Mobutu's case is perhaps the archetypal illustration of a corrupt leader. But it is far from uncommon: stories of large-scale corruption are reported on a regular basis in newspapers around the world. This is likely to be only the tip of the iceberg, with many cases left unreported at all levels of power.

Corruption is usually defined as any dishonest or illegal behavior, especially by those in power. It is most often associated with bribery, the act of offering something of value to someone for a favor, or embezzlement, the misappropriation of public or private assets placed in one's trust. But it can also take the form of collusion, which is the act of entering into a secret arrangement to take advantage of a market, such as price fixing, as well as nepotism, favoring friends and family. Whilst corruption can take place in both public and private sectors, it is more prevalent in the public sector. This is because the citizens of a country, which are the rightful owners of public goods, are too numerous and disseminated to properly safeguard their interests in those assets. Citizens are represented by institutions and public officials who may not take their fiduciary duty seriously, eager to benefit personally at the expense of the wider community.

That is not to say that the interests of private companies and those who manage them are always perfectly aligned, as various corporate scandals have shown. But they do tend to be better aligned, as private companies typically have more effective checks and balances in place than public ones. We should not conclude from these observations that all public assets should be privatized, but we should recognize that the potential for corruption is higher when public assets are involved.

The Trouble with Corruption

Corruption is undeniably detrimental to economic growth and to society in general. The allocation of resources in a corrupt society will be far from efficient, thus increasing costs. Those who end up in a position of power will be the ones who have bribed their way up or those who benefit from the best connections, not the ones with the best qualifications. In a corrupt society, business decisions are not made in the best interests of companies or their shareholders, but in the personal interests of those tasked with making those decisions. In poor countries, those receiving bribes rarely reinvest their ill-gotten gains into productive assets at home; funds are either spent on frivolous purchases or transferred out of the country. There are countless examples of corrupt political leaders and their entourage wasting public funds for personal gain.

This all comes at a cost. Former World Bank President Jim Yong Kim labelled corruption as the "largest single inhibitor of equitable economic development".[2] The overall cost of corruption is difficult to assess because of the difficulty in observing and measuring corruption. If, in a given country, few cases of corruption are reported, is it because there is little corruption or because those guilty of corruption are never prosecuted? Does the large increase of corruption cases in China in the past few years reflect a worrying trend or is it evidence that the crackdown is successful? Despite these uncertainties, what is clear is the large-scale corruption taking place around the world and its role as an impediment to growth.

In societies where corruption is endemic, those qualified for certain positions but without the ability to bribe or the right connections will be overlooked. They will feel a sense of injustice and unfairness, creating frustration and potentially leading to despair, violence, or unrest. It is no coincidence that countries with high levels of corruption are often those mired in conflicts.

Corruption and Social Trust

The most well-known measure of international corruption is the Corruption Perceptions Index (CPI) published by Transparency International, an international non-governmental organization which compiles an annual ranking of how corrupt each country is perceived to be. Because corruption is complex and difficult to detect (hence the inclusion of the word 'Perceptions'), the CPI has its critics, but overall, it is acknowledged as providing a fair assessment on the level of corruption around the world.

If we look at the ranking of each country in the CPI and compare that to the level of social trust in each of those countries (as measured by the World Values Survey), we find a remarkable correlation.[3] Nordic countries, the Netherlands, and Canada have the highest levels of social trust and are also the ones with the lowest perceived levels of corruption. These nations are certainly not immune to corrupt practices, but such practices are far less frequent. Conversely, countries with little trust in others tend to be perceived as the most corrupt.

When people generally trust each other, they tend to reject making gains or obtaining favors through dishonest means, even when given an opportunity to earn substantial gains with little risk of getting caught. That would go against the values they hold dear and which they were raised with. When researchers studied illegal parking fines from diplomats in New York, they found that diplomats from countries with high levels of perceived corruption (and low social trust) had accumulated the

most fines, whereas diplomats from Nordic countries and Japan had accumulated the fewest. Nordic or Japanese diplomats could have parked
illegally as their diplomatic immunity protects them from having to pay a
fine, yet they did not do so because such behavior goes against their values.[4] Diplomats from Kenya, for example, had no such qualms, collecting
many fines. Corruption in Kenya is pervasive to the point that getting a
job without a connection is almost impossible. A 2016 survey of young
people found that "half the respondents did not care how they made their
money, as long as they did not end up in jail" and that more than a third
would "easily give or take a bribe".[5]

Does higher social trust in a society make its citizens less corrupt or
does low corruption lead people to trust each other more? There is probably a bit of both, each reinforcing the other in a virtuous (or vicious)
cycle. But given the fact that social trust, like other human values, tends
to be stable over time, it is more likely for social trust to impact corruption
than the other way around.

The strong correlation between social trust and corruption does not
mean that countries with low social trust cannot fight corruption effectively. Botswana is an example of a nation with very low social trust that
is now considered, according to its CPI score, to be less corrupt than the
likes of Spain or Italy. Seretse Khama, the country's first president upon
independence, was uncompromising when it came to corruption. Drawing
his legitimacy not only from being competent and impartial but also as
the ruler of one of the main chieftaincies in the country, Khama understood that "corrupt practices were the ruin of Africa and had no place in
his thinly populated, impoverished, former protectorate".[6] He ensured
that offenders were swiftly brought to trial under an independent judici-
ary and dismissed from their positions if convicted, even when they
happened to be relatives or friends. Decisions such as the award of government contracts are made collegially, often by the entire cabinet, not
only the minister or official in charge. All budgets and development plan-
ning are openly debated, with communities and local governments
actively involved in the process. "All public spending projects have to
pass a dual hurdle of honesty and efficiency with honesty maintained by
rules of competitive tendering and efficiency enforced by careful technical scrutiny of the rate of return on each proposed project."[7]

Singapore is one of the least corrupt countries in the world, ranked fourth out of 180 countries in the latest CPI despite much lower levels of social trust compared to the other countries that make up the top 10.[8] It was not social trust that allowed it to fight corruption effectively. This was achieved solely through adequate policies: a leadership committed to tackling corruption, public servants selected solely on merit and paid competitively, strong penalties for those found guilty, swift dispensation of justice, minimal bureaucracy, and an effective anti-corruption agency. But the reality is that countries with low social trust will always find it more difficult to fight corruption than those where people generally trust each other. Only the implementation of a set of strong measures can change mentalities and have a real impact on corruption in low social trust nations, whereas countries with high levels of social trust can get away with low corruption more easily even when such measures are not in place.

Fighting Corruption

Once corruption sets in and becomes the accepted norm, it is very difficult to remove it. It pervades all aspects of society. Few countries have made real progress in reducing corruption once it has become endemic. China under Xi Jinping has made great strides but is hampered in its fight against corruption by the size of its public sector and an overall lack of transparency. The reason why it is so difficult to fight corruption, especially in countries with low social trust, is because once it sets in, everyone has an incentive to engage in such practices. If a job, promotion, or commercial contract can only be obtained by offering a bribe, those who refrain from it will miss out. Bribes become the only way of advancing one's career or conducting profitable business. It bleeds into every level and sector of society.

So, what is to be done? We explore here four measures that, in our view, are essential to effectively fight corruption: a real willingness *and* ability from top leaders to fight corruption; an effective rule of law which implies an independent anti-corruption agency and severe penalties handed out to those found guilty of corruption; providing credible alternatives to bribes; and higher transparency.

If change is to happen, it needs to come from the top: there needs to be genuine willingness by top political leaders to fight corruption. Leaders systematically claim that they will change the system, but they almost never do so because they themselves benefit greatly from it. Without the support from top leaders, any attempt to fight corruption is doomed to fail. Willingness to change the system is not enough; one must have the *ability* to do so. If a political leader genuinely wants to amend the system but is unable to proceed accordingly because he or she lacks the power to do so, not much will happen. Fighting corruption entails antagonizing powerful groups of interest, whether fellow politicians, army commanders, or private executives. Countless leaders have been overthrown or worse, paid with their lives for cracking down on corruption. Political leaders require strong legitimacy for such reforms to be pursued.

Assuming a leader has both the willingness and the ability to fight corruption, the next step will be to look at the incentives that drive people to engage in corrupt practices and reduce those incentives accordingly. Those offered a bribe will consider what they can gain from it but also what they could lose. If the expected benefits are high and the risks are low, people will be tempted to act accordingly, at least in a low social trust setting. To reduce that temptation, potential benefits should be lowered and risks significantly increased. In many countries, people feel they will never get caught, and even if they do, not much will happen to them. Increasing the risks means increasing the likelihood of getting caught and severely punishing those who do get caught. A Chinese public official may now think twice before giving or receiving a bribe if he knows that he has a good chance of getting caught, which would likely lead to a lengthy prison term and the end of his political career.

To catch offenders, a country requires an effective rule of law that provides a strong framework in which private property is upheld and transactions can be made where the rights and obligations of each party are clearly defined and enforceable. This includes setting up an anti-corruption agency, one which is independent, well-staffed, and well-budgeted. Independent means free of influence from public or private sources, including police forces. Any attempt by outsiders to influence the agency should be reported and severely dealt with. Well-staffed means staffed with competent employees. The best way to attract talent is to pay them well; if agency employees are underpaid, they themselves may fall victim to corruption. Well-budgeted means that the agency is sufficiently funded to conduct its investigations.

Once perpetrators are caught, they need to be put on trial and, if convicted, severely dealt with: the most serious crimes of corruption should be punished by several decades in jail. Even less serious crimes should still carry a punishment strong enough to act as a deterrent. This should reduce the incentive for people to act against the rules. Court cases need to be conducted swiftly, not after years of endless appeals or administrative processes. India had 6,502 pending cases at its anti-corruption agency at the end of 2016, of which 1,974 cases had been pending for more than 5 years, 1,424 for more than 10 years, and 209 for more than 20 years. Most trials last for years, sometimes decades. A third of high court judgeships remain vacant. There are only 19 judges for every million people, one of the lowest ratios in the world. The Delhi High Court calculated it would take 466 years to clear all the cases before the court.[9] Rather unsurprisingly, India ranks very low in the CPI rankings.[10]

The best way to reduce the benefits of accepting a bribe is to increase honest revenue streams. Too often, the salaries of top political leaders are ridiculously low to show proximity to the average citizen. But how can we expect these people, most of whom are well-educated and could obtain much better wages in the private sector, not to use their power to access illicit gains? The idea that political leaders go into politics for the sole purpose of serving their nation is idealistic (or truly exceptional). If they are underpaid, they will have every incentive to collect income through less scrupulous means. This is true of public officials at any level. Their wages need to reflect their level of qualification and competence, just as they do in the private sector. Doctors in China working in public hospitals often rely on 'gifts' by patients to compensate for their meager wages. Teachers in some developing countries require additional payments from parents. Officials could still collect bribes even if they are well-paid, but higher wages (and strong sanctions) reduce the likelihood that they would do so.

Transparency and accountability also play an important role. Those who take part in corrupt practices will want to keep it a secret. A transparent system makes it more likely that such practices are eventually disclosed. Nordic countries arguably have the most transparent systems in the world: the use of public funds is heavily scrutinized and citizens have access to information on public officials that would not be available elsewhere. A Scandinavian politician knows that engaging in corrupt practices is likely to be uncovered and that this would lead to a premature end to their political career, even if the amounts involved are small. Free press also contributes to higher transparency.

A great example of how transparency can reduce corruption in developing countries comes from Uganda. Ritva Reinikka and Jakob Svensson, two Swedish economists, studied an education grant program in which public funds were allocated to primary schools. They surveyed the schools to assess whether public funds had been received. It turned out that only 13 percent of the total grant had been received by schools, with most schools receiving nothing. The balance was kept by government officials and other intermediaries. Following the release of the study, the Ugandan government published monthly reports in local newspapers of how much school funding was allocated to each school district and requesting schools to report how much they had actually received. The increased transparency meant that intermediaries tasked with transferring the funds, such as local governments, would be caught in the act if they misappropriated those funds. Within a few years, 80 percent of all school funding reached the schools. Those schools with better access to newspapers recorded the most improvements.[11] This type of experiment deserves to be carried out in many more countries and sectors: whenever public funds are allocated to schools, hospitals, or other projects, surveys by an independent body should be conducted to assess how much each beneficiary actually receives compared to what they were supposed to receive. Any difference should only be caused by delays or a diversion of funds. Diverted funds should then be investigated and the culprits identified and brought to justice. There is no reason why the excellent results obtained in the Ugandan school experiment cannot be replicated elsewhere. Any leader who opposes such experiments is not taking the fight against corruption seriously.

Another obstacle to transparency is excessive red tape. Heavy bureaucracy makes it easier to find and exploit loopholes in the system and for abuses to remain undetected. In India, it was reported in 2013 that a senior police officer in the state of Karnataka was writing letters to himself. As inspector general for internal security, he had a duty to write letters to the inspector general for training. But because he oversaw both departments, the only way he could fulfill his responsibility was to write letters to himself and then reply to those letters. He commented that there were times when "he had to dictate a stern letter to himself because of the delay in response from himself from the other office".[12] This is not an isolated case. It takes, on average, 89 days to register a property and 10 years to close down a business. A manufacturing company is expected to comply with "seventy different laws, face multiple inspections, and file as many as 100 returns in a year."[13] In Japan, former public servant and journalist Aki Wakabayashi describes in her book how one day she was admonished by her employer "for saving her department ¥200 million [about US$1.8 million] — resulting in the danger of losing that amount in next year's budget. A mad rush ensues to spend the remainder of the budget before the impending fiscal year end: unneeded equipment is purchased, and a senior manager takes several favored female subordinates on a first-class trip around the world 'to study labor conditions in other countries'."[14] Bureaucracy should be reduced whenever possible to minimize opportunities for wrong doing.

Following the Right Examples

Corruption has derailed growth in many countries. Around the world and particularly in poor nations, it is one of the main concerns of populations tired of seeing their elites abusing their powers and misappropriating their nation's wealth. Those without money or connections have little hope of improving their living conditions in a system that, too often, is rigged against them.

Whilst it is difficult for low-trust societies to significantly curtail corruption, it is not an impossible task, as Botswana and others have shown. But it requires a series of measures to be put in place *concurrently*. Implementing only some of these measures and not others will not be sufficient. Societies that become more transparent and hand out strong punishments to those found guilty of corrupt acts will likely achieve little if their leaders are not serious about fighting corruption.

Unfortunately, few developing countries are prepared to go down that path. Whether they are elected or not, leaders too often have a vested interest in maintaining the status quo, making plenty of promises but delivering few. Malaysia's recent 1MDB (1Malaysia Development Berhad) scandal, in which billions of dollars of public funds were allegedly misappropriated to finance the lavish lifestyle of those tasked with managing those funds, serves as a reminder that Mobutu's excesses do not belong to an era long gone. There will undoubtedly be more Mobutus, ransacking their nation for personal gain at the expense of their population.

We began this chapter describing a country where corruption was and remains rampant. We conclude with another country on the same continent that has made great progress in its fight against corruption. Rwanda shares a border with the DRC, yet their policies have taken a very different turn in the past two decades. Under the leadership of Paul Kagame, Rwanda has enacted a series of reforms aimed at stamping out corruption. Whistleblowers are protected from prosecution, even those who have taken part in corrupt practices. Several high-ranking officials have been prosecuted and forced to resign in highly publicized corruption cases. According to Transparency International, the public procurement policy has been improved with higher transparency and stricter regulations. It is still in its early days, but those reforms have allowed Rwanda to quickly move up the CPI rankings, from 121st in 2006 to 51st in 2019. This trend is expected to continue. Leaders of developing countries would do well to follow in the footsteps of Botswana or Rwanda, with a genuine willingness to fight corruption and an ability to implement the right policies, providing hope to their people that they live in a fair society, and ultimately giving them a future they can look forward to.

Chapter 9

Fiscal Policy

As Romina finished up her dinner of chicken and potatoes she shared with her husband and their two children, she reflected on how their lives had changed in just over a year. They would never have been able to afford meat before; now they cooked chicken, goat, or pork at least twice a week. Their two children of six and eight years old now attended school every day. They would usually stop by a small store on their way back from school and buy cookies or fruits. They both looked in better health. Her husband was also doing better, drinking and smoking less. In the past year, she had been able to spend money on new clothes, shoes, healthier food, school supplies, and kitchen appliances, which meant that she no longer had to cook on the floor, with her husband occasionally providing a helping hand.

Romina and her family live in a small Peruvian village located in the remote district of Rosaspata, more than 2,000 miles above sea level in the Andes, a few miles away from the picturesque lake of Titicaca near the Bolivian border. What really changed since last year was the 100 soles (about US$30) Romina has been receiving from the government every month. US$30 a month may not seem much, but for impoverished families in Peru, it makes a big difference, sometimes doubling a family's income. The money went into Romina's newly-opened bank account, the very first time she held an account. The government had handed out cash in the past, but that had little impact on Romina and her family: her husband would simply pocket the money and use it mostly on drinks and cigarettes. The children were not going to school, instead staying at home and helping out with domestic chores. The family had also received food or medicine from the government, but only once or twice in a year. Deliveries were difficult in such a remote area and were often stolen by intermediaries. In those rare cases when food or medicine did reach Romina's family, they would be sold onwards to pay for daily expenses.

A major change has been the set of conditions that now had to be met for the money to be received. Romina and her children had to obtain identity cards. Her two children were required to attend school regularly, with teachers providing evidence to local authorities that this was indeed the case. Another requirement was that her children had to be vaccinated, as certified by a doctor. Romina is one of more than a million poor Peruvians (out of a total population of 28 million) that have benefited from a program called Juntos, or 'together' in Spanish, put in place by the government in September 2005. It was inspired by similar programs in Mexico and Brazil which have now spread across the continent and beyond. The aim of these *conditional cash transfers* is to incentivize beneficiaries to adopt a behavior conducive to further economic and social development. Cash is primarily given to mothers as women often make better use of it and tend to be more concerned about the welfare of their children. In the case of Juntos, the program covers impoverished households with children under the age of 14. Mothers have to sign an agreement of up to four years and ensure that children have a school attendance rate of at least 85 percent as evidenced by school records; complete all vaccinations; and, for children under three years old, use chlorinated water and anti-parasite medication. Pregnant women must attend both pre-natal and post-natal checks. Mothers also have to attend presentations by government officials that provide further information on Juntos and aim to promote better education and healthcare for their children. Cash transfers will be suspended for three months should these conditions not be met. If violations are still ongoing after three months, the program is terminated for the family.

Implementation of Juntos was not straightforward. Doctors dispatched to villages to assess compliance would be insulted and physically abused if they failed to provide their seal of approval. Teachers would sometimes collude with parents, stating that their children attended school when in fact they did not, or request bribes, knowing that parents were receiving monthly payments. Intermediaries would provide fake certificates of compliance. Monitoring was therefore essential to the success of the program. An independent department was put in place to oversee the implementation of Juntos and inspectors visited villages regularly to ensure compliance.

Peru has long been one of the most unequal countries in Latin America and, by extension, in the world. Back in 2005, two out of three children under the age of five lived below the poverty line, commonly defined in Peru as those belonging to households earning less than US$100 a month, often lacking access to education, water, electricity, or health services. Rural populations in particular suffered from armed conflict with a communist guerilla in the 1980s and 1990s, during which more than 60,000 people perished. Despite these setbacks, the results of the Juntos program have been nothing short of impressive: many more children enter and complete primary school, health services are more widely utilized and nutritional intake per household has improved, identity cards have enabled policymakers to better identify those households that require support and monitor the program, and income levels have improved, reducing inequalities significantly over the decade that followed the implementation of Juntos, an exceptional outcome in a world of rising inequalities.[1]

Taxing Inequalities

Inequality of both income and wealth have become a pressing issue of our times. Although there have been periods in history when inequalities were higher, most countries around the world have witnessed rising inequalities over the past 50 years. Globalization, a source of competition for low-skilled jobs in rich countries, market deregulation, the rise of the finance industry, and automation have all been blamed as factors leading to higher inequalities.

The widening gap between rich and poor is not so much because the poor are getting poorer. In most countries, their real (inflation-adjusted) income has either stagnated or increased slightly. It is the rich who are getting much richer, accumulating wealth on a scale not seen for a very long time. It could be argued that as long as the poor are not getting poorer, it does not really matter that the rich are getting richer; people should focus on what they have instead of what others have. But most of us do not think that way. We tend to define our happiness in relative terms, by looking at what others have in order to determine whether we should be contented with what we have. According to a United States (US) study, people would prefer to live in a neighborhood where they earn $50,000 whilst the average person earns $25,000, compared to one where they earn $100,000 whilst the average person earns $200,000.[2] Another US study found that if your neighbor has won the lottery, you are more likely to end up over-indebted or bankrupt because living next to rich people makes you spend more and incur more debt.[3] These results are hard to believe. Most of us are not conscious of the fact that we value what we earn and what we own in *relative* terms, not absolute ones. Economist Richard Easterlin puts it this way: "Imagine your income increases substantially while everyone else's stays the same — would you feel better off? The answer most people give is yes. But now, let's turn the example on its head. Think about a situation in which your real income stays the same, but everyone else's increases substantially — then how would you feel? Most people say that they would feel less well off, even though their real level of living hasn't, in fact, changed."[4] One factor that has made the wealth of others much more visible and displayed to wider audiences is social media. People tend to be selective in what they publish, boasting about their successes and hiding their failures, generating misconceptions among their audience about their true levels of wealth and happiness.

Widening income and wealth gaps often create a sense of unfairness. There is growing uneasiness with the fact that wealth is increasingly concentrated in the hands of a few people, at least in cases where those people are seen as undeserving of their wealth. Most of us have no issue with entrepreneurs such as Bill Gates earning billions: they built their companies from scratch, created thousands of jobs, and came up with products that are now widely used around the world. That seems fair. But hardly anyone will agree with Lehman Brothers ex-Chief Executive Officer Dick Fuld pocketing US$500 million of income from 2000 to 2007 before running his company to the ground and contributing to a crisis that required US$700 billion of US taxpayer money. Some people will have earned their wealth through hard work; others will have inherited it, accumulating it further without putting in much effort. Personal connections often act as a shortcut to landing a well-paying job or a lucrative contract.

This feeling of unfairness manifests itself in everyday life: when reading about company executives earning millions, seeing a sports car whiz by, or walking past first class seats on your way to your cramped economy seat for that 10-hour overnight flight (a US study found that passengers walking through first class on their way to economy class are three times more likely to get into an air rage compared to those entering the plane directly into economy class).[5] This sense of unfairness is not always justified. Most people will agree that in a meritocratic society, those who work hard and hold positions of high responsibilities should earn more. A chief executive officer should earn more than her colleagues given her level of responsibilities. Some level of inequality will be inevitable, particularly in fast-rising economies where wealth first needs to be created before it can be distributed. But growing inequalities are becoming a growing issue.

One of the main instruments at the disposal of policymakers to tackle inequality is fiscal policy, and more particularly tax policy. The solution seems obvious: higher taxes. The higher the taxes, especially when they apply to the wealthy and high-income earners, the more the state can redistribute to those who have less. This should logically reduce the gap between the rich and poor. Proponents of higher taxes point to Nordic countries. They have very high taxes, their economies are doing well, and inequalities are kept low. Scandinavians enjoy a high social safety net in the form of generous unemployment, healthcare, education, and retirement benefits. Why can other countries not simply replicate that model?

Some have tried. In most cases, it did not end well. As taxes were raised to much higher levels, companies and wealthy individuals started leaving the country, whilst those who remained came up with ingenious ways to evade taxes. So-called 'tax optimization' advisers would suddenly find themselves in high demand. Some workers would become less dedicated to their task: why bother working hard if most of their income is paid to the state and they can earn almost as much by collecting subsidies? In the end, tax income hardly increases; in some cases, it even shrinks.

There comes a point, which appears to be different in every country, where raising the tax rate further results in lower tax revenues. In the western world, the marginal tax rate that maximizes tax revenue is estimated to be between 50 and 60 percent.[6] Beyond that, tax revenues drop.

In 2013 French President François Hollande introduced a 75 percent top tax rate for those earning more than one million euros. During 2013 and 2014, the two fiscal years when the new tax was implemented, only 260 million and 160 million euros of additional tax revenues were collected, respectively.[7] Businesses were transferring their activities to other countries. Foreign investors were pulling out. A few high-profile individuals decided to emigrate, among them Bernard Arnault, France's richest man, who took Belgian citizenship. On a lighter note, even professional soccer players threatened to go on strike, though their plight attracted little sympathy. Over the same period, the budget deficit soared to new highs. The French government quickly backtracked: the new tax was scrapped less than two years after it was introduced. Similar scenarios played out in other countries that attempted to significantly raise their tax rates.

Trust and Tax

Why do some countries succeed at raising taxes whilst others do not?

To answer this question, let us begin with an easier one: why do people pay taxes? Most of us pay taxes because we do not have a choice. If we do not pay taxes, we expose ourselves to penalties ranging from fines to jail or even death, depending on the jurisdiction that applies and the severity of the crime. If given a choice, many of us would opt not to pay *any* tax. But for some people, there is another reason why they pay tax. If they trust others in paying their fair share of taxes and they trust their political institutions in doing a good job managing tax revenues and redistributions, they will find it *fair* to pay at least *some* tax. For them, taxes are perceived as a legitimate and necessary tool for governments to better manage the economy.

If, on the other hand, governments fail to handle tax revenues properly by siphoning funds for personal gain, investing in unproductive assets, or using funds to pay for a bloated bureaucracy, people will not trust their government. Similarly, if they observe that others are not paying their fair share of tax or abuse social benefits, the state will not be considered as a legitimate tax collector and when that happens, people resort to unproductive behavior such as tax evasion or shirking work, which ultimately weigh on the economy. Trust therefore determines, to a large extent, the level of taxation that a country is able to adopt. Simply put, if people do not trust each other or their government, taxes should be kept low, even if that comes at the expense of widening inequalities. But if people do trust each other and their government, taxes should be higher so that inequalities can be contained.

If we compare the level of tax revenues in a given country, measured by the tax-to-GDP (gross domestic product) ratio to the level of social trust, measured by surveys, we find a strong relationship: countries with high tax rates are also the ones where people trust each other the most. One study found that companies in countries with higher social trust are less likely to resort to tax avoidance schemes.[8] But countries where people have little trust for others are often those with the lowest tax revenues.[9] These results indicate that some countries have tax levels that may be too low given their level of social trust. China, Mexico, and the US would appear to have room to increase their tax rates to reduce inequalities.

The above is not to say that countries with high levels of social trust can raise taxes indefinitely. When Sweden, a nation where trust in others and in political institutions is among the highest in the world, raised its income tax rates at the end of the 1970s up to 85 percent for some of its top earners, economic growth slowed considerably, public deficits soared, and tax revenues grew only marginally when the government had expected a much higher tax windfall. Wealthy individuals, among which IKEA founder Ingvar Kamprad, Tetra Pak founder Ruben Rausing, industrialist Fredrik Lundberg, film producer Ingmar Bergman, and tennis player Björn Borg, started leaving the country. If low inequalities are the result of high-income earners leaving the country, this is hardly a desirable outcome. Local companies struggled under the tax strain and productivity fell. Even doctors began working part-time as they would not earn more, after deducting taxes, if they worked longer. Sweden had to reverse course a few years later. The best evidence that very high taxes were not working out as intended is how little they contributed to Swedish finances. At best, inheritance and capital gain taxes contributed 0.4 percent of annual GDP each. When they were both scrapped in 2004 and 2007, respectively, they were contributing less than 0.2 percent of annual GDP each. People were evidently finding ways around them.

In this chapter, we have thus far discussed taxation in general terms. There are, of course, various types of personal and corporate taxes, including indirect ones such as value-added tax or export taxes. Emerging markets have more indirect taxes as a percentage of total tax revenues than developed nations as indirect taxes are easier to collect and monitor, especially for economies with a large informal sector. Some income tax systems are more progressive than others, placing a heavier burden on higher income earners. Although we should be mindful of these considerations, the fact that we have not gone into the specifics of various tax systems should not invalidate the general conclusion that social trust matters greatly and that higher social trust allows for higher overall levels of taxation, which in turn contribute to lower inequalities of income and wealth.

Too often the debate on taxation is ideological, between those on the political right who vehemently oppose any tax increase because they see it as government interference that infringes on the freedom of citizens or creates unnecessary distortions in the economy, and those on the political left who systematically push for higher taxes as a means to greater social justice. Both are highly simplistic and erroneous views: high taxes make sense in some societies but not in others.

Welfare Spending: Beyond Stereotypes

In the previous section, we explored how governments collect revenues, mostly in the form of taxes. We now focus on how governments actually spend those revenues. Although there are many ways to do so, our focus here is on the one expenditure that has risen the most in the past 50 years and which now represents the highest single expenditure for many countries: social benefits. Nations, especially western ones, have devoted an increasingly high portion of their budget to cater to those with low income, retirees, children, the unemployed, or those who require medical assistance. Although large differences persist, with some low-income countries spending as little as 5 percent of their budget on social spending whilst others spend as much as 50 percent or more, the global trend is geared towards more social spending.

As they do when it comes to taxes, most people have an ideological, simplistic view of public social spending. Consider the following two examples.

The past year has been tough for Adam, an information technology (IT) specialist in his fifties. Six months ago, he lost his job as his company, a consultancy, closed down amidst a severe slowdown in demand for IT services. Since then, he has sent his resume to over 100 potential employers, in each case receiving negative feedback despite being flexible in terms of salary, location, and scope of work. The economic outlook is rather bleak at the moment and few companies are hiring, with many of them having outsourced or off-shored positions to lower-cost countries. The few companies still hiring would rather employ a fresh graduate with a few years of experience rather than a middle-aged person who has been out of a job for six months. This seems unfair to Adam: he is hard-working and competent at what he does; he just needs to be given a chance to prove himself again. He is growing rather disillusioned with this turn of events. A complicated divorce last year has compounded the issues he is facing. Thankfully, he can rely on unemployment benefits, without which he would really struggle. This has greatly helped him go through a situation that he hopes is only temporary.

Brian is in his early thirties. He has never worked much in his life and has no intention of doing so anytime soon. He spends most of his days playing video games and having drinks with his friends, many of whom share his philosophy of life. He never quite understood why people enslave themselves at work in an endless pursuit of materialistic gain, never seeming satisfied with their own lives. He relies on generous welfare packages which allow him to live relatively comfortably. Sure, that pesky counsellor at the unemployment office forces him to attend a few job interviews each year. But he always makes sure he fails them and has so far gotten away with it. He might consider working a little, but only if the job provides flexible hours and is located within walking distance to where he lives.

Adam and Brian are stereotypes. Although there are many Adams and Brians in this world, they represent two extremes in a wide range of attitudes a person may adopt. Yet many of us believe that people are almost entirely comprised of either Adams or Brians. This is often a result of our ideological mindset. Those on the political right tend to view the unemployed as a lazy bunch who abuse generous welfare systems. Those on the political left tend to view the unemployed as hard-working people who have become victims to a malfunctioning system. These antagonistic views differ significantly between countries. When asked whether people who require social assistance end up in such a situation because of laziness and a lack of willpower or because of an unfair society, 60 percent of Americans believe it is because of laziness and a lack of willpower, whereas only 39 percent of Germans believe that to be the case.[10]

One reason for such gaps in perception is the difficulty in having reliable data on how people actually behave. Those who behave like Brian will typically not boast about the fact that they are not trying very hard to find a job. In the absence of reliable data, we instead rely on our personal experiences to form our opinions. We observe certain people and may deduce that their behavior reflects the aggregate behavior of all citizens. This can be misleading as our personal observations may not be representative of an entire society. Yet these perceptions, however inaccurate they may be, have far-reaching consequences. If policymakers believe most people to behave like Brian, they will reduce benefits in the hope that this will entice those without a job to look for one more actively. If, on the contrary, they believe most people behave like Adam, benefits will be maintained or increased to support those in a precarious but temporary situation, believing that cutting benefits would only create further hardship on beneficiaries. Policymakers should strive to find the right balance, one that reduces the incentive for people to abuse benefits whilst at the same time providing adequate levels of social protection to those who need it.

Similar to taxation, social trust plays an important role in the way we approach social benefits. In societies where people generally trust each other, more will behave like Adam. Few will try to game the system. Nordic countries provide generous social benefits, whether they cover unemployment, education, retirement, or medical services. Yet few people abuse the system; many would be embarrassed to do so. They would not do it even if they knew they could get away with it. But in countries where people generally do not trust each other, more end up behaving like Brian, having no qualms about taking advantage of the system.

Reducing Inequalities in Countries with Low Social Trust

We have so far outlined how the redistributive role of the state can be expanded in countries with high social trust by increasing taxes and social benefits, and ultimately reducing inequalities. But what about countries where social trust is low? Are those nations doomed to have permanently high levels of inequality?

Some approaches do not work. Increasing social trust is not an option: people will not suddenly become more trusting of others. Focusing solely on the rich also does not work: no country with low social trust has ever managed to sustainably reduce inequalities simply by taxing the rich more. This Robin Hood fantasy may appeal to an electorate but does not work in the real world because most of the wealthy and high-earners are sufficiently ingenious to circumvent higher taxes. One caveat to this state-ment is the introduction of tax reporting by third parties, such as employ-ers, but also credit card providers or banks. Rather than solely relying on the tax declaration of individual workers, tax authorities may require employers to report the income levels of employees directly to these authorities. Unless there is collusion between employee and employer, this reporting system makes it more difficult to evade taxes. It is, however, much less efficient in societies in which many taxpayers are self-employed, which is the case for poorer countries.

Rather than focusing on the rich, countries with little social trust should instead focus on the poor and aim to lift them out of poverty. Doing so requires giving them the right incentives, either by 'nudging' them or forcing them to adopt a certain desired behavior. One of the most success-ful applications of behavioral finance has been in relation to retirement savings. In many countries, employees have some flexibility in terms of how much they contribute to their retirement savings. But most people do not worry much about setting aside sufficient funds for their retirement, especially when that retirement is far into the future. A 30-year-old will usually not give much thought about what his financial situation might be when he retires 35 years or so later. This can be a costly mistake: saving early on in life does make a big difference towards a comfortable retirement, owing to the power of compounding interest. To entice people to save more for their retirement, economists Richard Thaler and Shlomo Benartzi devised a system whereby employees are automatically enrolled to have a portion of their *future* wage increases to be deposited into a savings account. Employees can opt out of the scheme, but very few actually do. Savings rates increased dramatically wherever this was implemented: even people who are unwilling to save more today will have fewer qualms about doing so in the future.[11]

Conditional Cash Transfers

Another powerful scheme to get people out of poverty in countries with low social trust has been conditional cash transfers (CCTs), which originated in Latin America, a region where social trust is exceptionally low. Unsurprisingly, this is also a region with highly unequal societies, the most unequal in the world by most accounts. But since 2000, income inequalities have unexpectedly *declined*. Even more unexpectedly, this has happened in almost all Latin American countries. The various policies put in place by governments across the political spectrum made little difference. This is a remarkable result. In a world where inequalities continue to grow, Latin America is the only region where inequalities have actually decreased.[12]

Several explanations have been put forth. One is the prolonged period of economic growth that the region enjoyed from 2000 to 2010. Yet other countries in the world that experienced similar growth had seen income inequalities *widen*, not reduce. Why would Latin America be any different? Another explanation is the increase of tax revenues. It is true that tax revenues as a proportion of GDP have gone up in most countries in the region since 2000. But this is not so much the result of higher individual tax rates; it has more to do with improved market conditions, in particular the commodity boom that has benefited many countries in the region. Furthermore, sales and export taxes in Latin American governments represent a much higher proportion of taxes collected compared to OECD (Organisation for Economic Co-operation and Development) countries. Indirect taxes do not reduce inequalities, on the contrary, they represent a higher burden for those with lower income. Latin American governments also rely more heavily on corporate rather than individual tax income.[13] Income inequality has not been reduced because of a transfer of wealth from the rich to the poor. In fact, the rich have continued to become richer. From 2002 to 2015, the wealth of Latin American billionaires is estimated to have grown by an average of 21 percent *each year*, 6 times greater than the growth of GDP for the region.[14] Inequalities were reduced because the conditions of the poor and the middle class improved, in large part as a result of the implementation of conditional cash transfers.

Before CCTs were introduced at the end of the 1990s, social benefits were distributed in cash or in kind to those below a predetermined income threshold. The effectiveness of these policies was limited at best and counterproductive at worst, with some beneficiaries abusing benefits (in other words, behaving like Brian). As described in the case of Peru and its Juntos program, CCTs were introduced to provide cash to poor families, subject to certain conditions being met. This proved particularly effective with rural families that relied on children for additional income. Under the old system, families would collect cash from the government but still deny their children access to school, even when school attendance was free, depriving them of a potentially brighter future. But with CCTs, parents no longer had that option: if they wanted a cash handout, their children had to attend school.

Given its success, CCTs quickly spread across the region. It is estimated that in 2011, as many as 129 million people, mostly low-income families, were benefiting from CCTs in Latin America.[15] This number can only have grown since then. One study found that from 1995 to 2005, CCTs reduced inequalities by 21 percent in Brazil and Mexico and 15 percent in Chile.[16] Another study concluded that poverty in the region would have been 13 percent higher if CCTs had not been implemented.[17] Other countries in the world have since introduced CCTs: in South Asia, Africa, and elsewhere. More nations should follow this path, including those that have already reached a high level of development but where social trust remains low.

Chapter 10

Monetary Policy

If Zimbabwean television had hosted a national version of the popular show *Who Wants to be a Millionaire?* back in 2008, contestants would be aiming to earn hundreds of *trillions* of Zimbabwean dollars to make it worthwhile; one million dollars would not even be sufficient to purchase a cup of coffee. Contestants would also be faced with a challenge that fellow participants around the world did not need to worry about: answering questions correctly as quickly as possible. The longer it took them to answer questions, the lower their earnings would be worth in a country where the value of money diminished by the hour. Prices doubled almost every day. Bus drivers were charging commuters more in the evening than in the morning and changing local notes into foreign currency three times a day. In the capital Harare, money dealers could be found around most street corners.[1]

Back in the late 1990s and early 2000s, President Robert Mugabe's government embarked on a series of reforms that ultimately bankrupted the country. Public companies were set up in various sectors and ran by unqualified political cronies. Most would end up accumulating large losses and requiring further funding from the government to stay afloat. Land reforms were enacted, redistributing land to those who had little experience running a farm. That led to a collapse in agriculture production, forcing the country to import food and depriving it of foreign reserves. The banking sector crumbled, most people became unemployed, and even life expectancy declined. Undeterred, the government kept on spending. It also participated in a military conflict in the neighboring Democratic Republic of the Congo. All this costs money, which the state no longer had.

Out of cash but not out of ideas, the government instructed the central bank to create more money. To Zimbabwean policymakers, it felt like an easy solution: creating money to pay off debts and cover expenses. The governor of Zimbabwe's central bank, Gideon Gono, who would regularly implore God during public speeches to ensure the successful implementation of his policies, felt that "traditional economics do not fully apply in this country".[2] He would soon be proven wrong. With so much new money coming into circulation and hardly any of it utilized for productive purposes, at some point the value of that money inevitably decreases. Workers (at least those who still had a job), expecting even higher prices in the future, demanded higher wages. Faced with higher wages, companies had to increase the prices of the goods they sold. Prices reached record highs in an ever-increasing spiral. Gono would be seen on the streets of Harare begging shop owners to drop their prices. Alas, neither them nor the Lord were willing to entertain his pleas.

The worthless currency was eventually discontinued and replaced by foreign money, mostly US dollars and South African rands. But even then, banks had to place heavy restrictions on the amount of money that people could withdraw: without such restrictions, most people would withdraw all their money at once, having little trust in local banks. After a decade without its own currency, Zimbabwe introduced a new Zimbabwe dollar in 2019. Although the central bank is now (officially at least) more cautious about printing money and has increased interest rates to 50 percent, prices are once again on the rise, increasing at a rate that would make them more than double every year. Zimbabweans simply have no confidence in the ability of their leaders to stabilize the currency after years of economic mismanagement. Once confidence is lost, it is very difficult to regain it. The latest move by the government, the decision in August 2019 to withhold the publication of monthly prices for several months, will do nothing to improve confidence in the new currency.[3]

Monetary Policies Around the World

Despite efforts over the past decades to make it more transparent and accountable, the monetary policy is often seen as obscure, perhaps even mystical. Central bankers use a jargon barely perceptible to those who are not actively involved in that field. The concept of money, how it is created, how it flows through the banking system and the wider economy, and how it impacts economic indicators such as inflation, gross domestic product, exchange rates, or the unemployment rate can be rather confusing. Yet the importance of monetary policy to an economy cannot be overstated. A misguided policy may lead to much higher prices, lower growth, currency instability, or a malfunctioning financial sector, all of which can result in crises with devastating consequences, even destroying entire economies as the case of Zimbabwe has all too clearly demonstrated.

Central bankers have a number of tools at their disposal to regulate money and banking. The effectiveness of those tools will be different in each country depending on the structure of their economy. In countries with high savings rates and a reliance on exports for growth, a key consideration will be the exchange rates those nations have with their main trading partners: a stronger local currency will make exports more expensive and therefore less attractive, whereas a weaker currency will make those exports more competitive. This is particularly true of economies with a more limited domestic market such as Singapore, Hong Kong, or Switzerland. Preventing the local currency from becoming too strong is usually done by increasing foreign currency reserves.[4] The top 10 economies with the highest foreign reserves as of January 2020 all either have a thrifty population or large commodity producers: mainland China, Japan, Switzerland, Russia, Saudi Arabia, Taiwan, Hong Kong, India, South Korea, and Brazil.[5] Another reason for holding large foreign currency reserves is to avoid speculative attacks or sudden withdrawals by foreign investors that can destabilize the local currency, especially when it is pegged to another currency or a basket of currencies. This was the case during the 1997 Asian financial crisis when the currencies of Thailand, Indonesia, and South Korea, to name those economies most severely affected by the crisis, saw their values plunge as foreign investors exited the region in droves. More recently, the large withdrawals of money from emerging markets in 2018 as foreign investors repatriated their funds resulted in many currencies suffering sharp declines, undermining their credibility.

Monetary authorities in countries with large domestic markets, especially those with low savings rates and a low reliance on exports for their growth, will be more focused on short-term interest rates. Even then, currency exchange rates do matter, and matter more than they used to in an increasingly globalized world. But under normal circumstances, they would not be the main driver of monetary policy for those countries.

Not all countries benefit from well-functioning capital markets. In such cases, one instrument available to central banks is to adjust the reserve requirements on commercial banks, forcing banks to hold a certain portion of their liabilities with the central bank in the form of reserves. Because traditional banks lend more than the deposits they hold and use short-term deposits to finance longer-term loans, reserve requirements act as a safety buffer by ensuring that banks do not become reckless in their lending practices and potentially run out of cash. Reserve requirements are largely outdated in many countries that use other regulatory and supervisory instruments to monitor the reserves held by commercial banks, but they remain an important monetary tool in countries with more limited capital markets, as well as those that have made the decision to use reserve requirements as one of their main monetary tools, such as China.

Too often, leaders of poor countries have a very weak understanding of the role money and banking have within their economies. This lack of understanding sometimes even extends to central bankers, who ought to know better. This can result in policies that are not in the best interests of their citizens; few Zimbabweans would disagree with this statement. It is therefore essential to hire the right people to manage monetary policies and let them get on with their job, free from political interference. If the right candidates cannot be found within the country, outsiders should be considered. Practical experience in a reputable foreign central bank, even for just a few months, should be a prerequisite. Central bankers around the world, but particularly in poorer nations rife with corruption, should be adequately compensated given their level of responsibilities so that their country can retain them, but also to safeguard their independence and their integrity.

Inflation

Price stability constitutes the main mandate given to central banks around the world. Price inflation, or simply inflation, refers to the increase in the price of goods and services affecting households. High inflation distorts prices, creates confusion, and, if left unchecked, feeds on itself in ever-increasing numbers. But inflation which is too low or even negative may push people to postpone their consumption, reducing growth. Too high or too low inflation is therefore undesirable. Most central banks in developed economies target an inflation rate of around two percent; this is usually higher in developing countries that are expected to generate higher levels of nominal (pre-inflation) growth.

Inflation, in the absence of price controls and other rigidities, is determined by the supply and demand of the goods and services that make up an inflation index. There are many reasons why prices may go up or down, some of them monetary in nature and others not. If a supply shortfall increases the price of oil and oil is a component of the inflation index, inflation will increase. If the economy experiences a downturn, demand for goods and services decreases, and prices will not rise as much as before (or even drop). Over longer periods of time, prices tend to reflect the amount of money that circulates in an economy: any increase in the money supply not absorbed by economic activity will eventually be reflected in higher prices.

The inflation rate is closely related to wages and the unemployment rate. If the economy is doing well and few people are without a job, there will be less competition for each job and companies will find it more difficult to hire. Workers will ask for, and often obtain, higher wages. With higher wages, they are able to spend more, boosting demand for goods and services, and therefore increasing prices. But if there are many people without a job, businesses can afford to be more selective in their hiring and provide less attractive wages. Workers will not earn as much and spend less, reducing demand for goods and services, and therefore reducing prices (or increasing them at a lower rate). The implication for central banks is that unemployment can be lowered but at the expense of higher inflation.

There is, of course, one important case where the relation between inflation and unemployment breaks down. When people expect future prices and wages to go up, inflation may pick up without any corresponding decrease in unemployment. In such a scenario, workers start to factor future price increases into their wages; companies, faced with higher production costs, reflect those costs in the selling price of their products or services. Inflation expectations become self-fulfilling, irrespective of the state of the job market or the wider economy. Inflation takes a life of its own. Any attempts to lower the unemployment rate below what would be considered as the full employment rate will not succeed, or only in a temporary capacity. Full employment does not mean that everyone has a job, as some workers will be in-between jobs and others may lack the required skills to fill vacancies. It is a theoretical rate because no one really knows what that rate actually is. But the consequences of breaching that rate are anything but theoretical. A central bank that reduces interest rates in order to lower the unemployment rate below the full employment rate is likely to trigger inflation expectations. Workers will ask for higher wages as they expect future prices to go up. Companies faced with higher labor costs will generate lower margins and may have to reduce their workforce. As a result, the unemployment rate reverts back to its original level. The initial decline in short-term interest rates and the corresponding increase in the money supply would have generated higher inflation and possibly reduced economic activity without any long-term improvement in the unemployment rate.

When do people start expecting future prices to go up? At low levels of inflation, most of us will barely notice it. If our wages increased by three percent this year, whereas the increase was only one percent the previous year, we feel better off compared to the previous year. But that should not always be the case. If inflation reached two percent last year and was flat this year, we would have received the same *real* annual wage increase of one percent over those two years. What we have failed to realize is that the *value* of our earnings last year was eroded by two percent. Countless psychological studies have shown how people are affected by money illusion, the inability to fully take inflation into account.[6] In a United States (US) survey, half of all respondents would feel more satisfied about their job if their pay went up even if prices went up as much. Not only do most people not realize how inflation affects their purchasing power, they also fail to acknowledge how higher prices impact the economy, including their own income. When asked whether their income in the past five years would have been higher if inflation had been higher during that period compared to no inflation at all, only a third of respondents thought that this would indeed be the case.[7]

At some point, people start to realize that something is wrong, that the value of their income and savings is being depleted. They start to form expectations about future prices and behave accordingly.[8] If prices increase by 10 percent every year, people will want that increase to be reflected in their wages. The question then becomes: at what rate do people start forming expectations about future prices and using them in their decision-making process? Economists George Akerlof, William Dickens, and George Perry published a paper in 2000 describing how in the US, people only start forming (and using) inflation expectations as the Consumer Price Index, the most common proxy for inflation in the US, exceeds 3.5 percent.[9] Below that level, people fail to take inflation into account and act upon it. If this holds true, the implication for monetary policy is that at low levels of inflation, interest rates can be pushed lower than what is conventionally assumed, resulting in higher employment and growth without triggering higher inflation. An inflation target of two percent may therefore be too low and prevents the economy from reaching its full potential. A target of three percent would be more appropriate, bearing in mind that any inflation that rises above that number will likely trigger inflation expectations that then become very difficult to reverse. Another implication is that attempting to reduce inflation below two percent, in the hope that an ensuing economic downturn will only be temporary as the unemployment rate eventually reverts back to its full employment rate, is a misguided policy; without people forming inflation expectations at low levels of inflation and unwilling to reduce their nominal wages, the resulting higher unemployment rate could remain high for much longer.

Fighting High Inflation

Once high inflation expectations set in, reverting back to lower levels of inflation becomes a real challenge. The most common and intuitive solution is to reduce the amount of money in circulation (or, in extreme cases, replace the currency). This normally takes the form of higher interest rates, higher reserve requirements for commercial banks, or the appreciation of the local currency for those nations that rely heavily on exports for growth (typically by converting foreign currency reserves into local currency). These measures are likely to lead to reduced economic activity and higher unemployment: higher interest rates increase the cost of borrowing, higher reserve requirements reduce the ability of banks to lend, and a stronger local currency makes exports less competitive. But an economic downturn, even a severe one, may be necessary for inflation expectations to be quelled before the economy can bounce back. To have any chance of succeeding, the actions taken by the central bank have to be viewed as *credible*. If people and businesses do not believe that the central bank is resolute in its determination to fight inflation, inflation expectations will not subside.

Unfortunately, few countries, rich or poor, are willing to undergo a (potentially prolonged) period of hardship. Politicians with control over monetary matters, who are up for re-election, or at risk of being deposed in a military coup will be reluctant to impose temporary hardship on their citizens. Fighting high inflation works best in countries where the central bank is independent from political interference. In the 1970s, there was a push in the western world for more independence for central banks as nations experienced high inflation and politicians were pushing back on attempts to increase interest rates. But in many countries (even rich ones), central banks are far from independent and even those which are have to continuously defend their independence. In the absence of a truly independent central bank, it is up to political leaders to take the courageous decision to limit economic growth for the short term in exchange for longer-term prosperity. This is more easily done in politically stable regimes where leaders do not have to fear being removed from office, whether because of elections or military action. But it still requires a willingness and ability to do the right thing. So far, China has successfully put the brakes on an economy that, at times, was at risk of overheating despite a central bank that takes its instructions from political leaders. But overall, political willingness to fight high inflation in developing countries is often lacking.

Another option to fight high inflation is price controls (or less commonly, wage controls). In this scenario, the government fixes or limits the rise of certain prices. This often requires subsidies to producers who have to sell at below market prices. Price controls can apply to any item that affects the budget of households: fuel, bread, sugar, healthcare costs, even mobile phones or television subscriptions. At first this may seem like a good idea as it provides a quick fix to rising prices. But it often comes at a terrible cost. Countries that have experimented with price controls often struggle with state coffers becoming rapidly depleted because of the generous subsidies. If subsidies are kept too low, producers could go bust and will have little incentive to produce at a loss, leading to shortages. Price distortions also lead to the emergence of a black market, especially in countries with high corruption levels.

There are, however, cases where price controls may be justified. Necessity goods such as bread, rice, or fuel are often heavily subsidized in developing countries to ensure affordability to those with low income. Inflation can also be imported if the cost of imported goods increases because of higher international prices or a weaker local currency. When the cost of imported basic necessity goods rises, this creates hardship. One way to counteract the impact of imported inflation is to have state-owned intermediaries handle the import of products or services at market prices and sell them domestically at subsidized prices. Those intermediaries will incur a loss as a result, but that may be a preferable outcome compared to a general rise in prices. China is one country that has, in the past, resorted to such temporary measures for the import of certain commodities. Although price controls may be justified in those cases, they should be temporary and need to be closely monitored as the market distortions they generate can lead to abuse.

Employment in the Age of the Gig Economy

While high inflation threatens growth and stability in developing countries, high-income nations are having to grapple with the opposite problem: too *low* inflation. Over the last decade, central bankers continuously believed (and many still do) that record low unemployment rates would lead to higher wages and higher inflation. They would rely on historical models predicting that unemployment rates of three to four percent would inevitably result in increased wages and prices. Fear of higher inflation justified raising interest rates at the expense of further growth. Yet wages and inflation have remained stubbornly low. By the end of 2019, before the Covid-19 pandemic, the unemployment rate had reached historical lows in many rich nations: in the US, it was the lowest in 60 years; in the United Kingdom (UK), the lowest since 1975; in Germany, the lowest since 1990; and in Japan, the lowest in 25 years. All this fear about robots and automation causing massive unemployment has, at least so far, not materialized, far from it in fact.

The reason why record low unemployment is not causing higher wages and higher inflation is that the structure of the job market has undergone fundamental changes. The unemployment rate has historically been an indicator of 'slack' in the labor market. A very low unemployment rate meant that few people were competing for the same jobs, forcing companies to raise wages to attract workers from other employers. But over the past decade, many people were without a full-time, well-paying job *despite* record low unemployment rates. They had either given up on finding a job because they just could not find one or were working on a part-time basis, unable to secure a *good* job: one that pays well, is full-time, and corresponds to the qualifications of workers. Many have become *underemployed*. This is evident when we look at levels of employment: the number of people with a job compared to the working age population. The employment rate has declined significantly since the 2008 financial crisis, especially in the US.[10]

Why are there so many workers not considered as unemployed but still unable to secure good jobs? This is sometimes explained by strong competition for low-skilled jobs from other countries, increased migration, widening inequalities, and higher homeownership. These factors probably play a role, but they have done so over decades and could not, by themselves, fully explain the rise of underemployment in the past decade. Consider instead the following (pre-Covid-19) numbers. Lyft, the largest US ride-sharing application, has 1.5 million active drivers in the country. Uber, its closest rival, has 900,000 active drivers in the country (and 3 million globally). Didi Chuxing, the biggest ride-sharing platform in China, has a massive 30 million active drivers using its platform. Airbnb, another platform that allows hosts to accommodate guests for short-term stays against a fee, has more than six million listings on its website. Grubhub, the largest food delivery service in the US, processes more than 400,000 orders each *day* through its network of drivers.[11] These jobs did not exist 10 years ago. Most of us associate the gig economy with these companies. But they only represent a small fraction of it. It is not only about drivers, food deliveries, or house rentals. Consultants, freelance writers, independent lawyers, laundry home pick-up and delivery, and renting car space with empty seats for long trips are all examples of gig work. There are even platforms that will walk your dog for a fee or come to the rescue of those suffering from arachnophobia when a spider is found in their home.

In the US at the end of 2019, one percent of unemployed workers represented about 1.6 million people, slightly less than all active Lyft drivers.[12] This gives us an idea of the impact that the gig economy is having on US employment and why so many jobs were lost during the Covid-19 pandemic. Of course, many drivers work for multiple platforms, may rent their apartment for a few days, and deliver food on another work shift. These jobs are not always newly-created ones: a number of traditional taxi drivers have probably been replaced by Lyft or Uber drivers, or may have transitioned themselves to those platforms. But the sheer size of those new companies and the number of workers using their platforms is evidence that many new jobs have been created. The true impact of the gig economy remains difficult to assess. Should all part-time or short-term jobs be considered part of the gig economy? What about full-time workers who also have a part-time job, such as those who drive for Uber over weekends for extra income? One study in the US found that the number of 'traditional', full-time jobs did not increase between 2005 and 2015. Almost all newly-created jobs during that period came through 'alternative work arrangements', which the authors define as "temporary help agency workers, on-call workers, contract company workers, and independent contractors or freelancers". This is very much a new phenomenon: from 1995 to 2005, the authors of the study point out that those alternative work arrangements had almost no impact on the growth of jobs in the US economy.[13] Gallup, a consultancy, using a broad definition of gig work, estimates that a staggering 57 million American workers, or 36 percent of the working-age population, now work in the gig economy.[14] The Federal Reserve finds similar, albeit slightly lower numbers.[15] The Bureau of

Labor Statistics sees a much lower figure, estimating that 10 percent of US workers were employed in alternative work arrangements.[16] Whatever the true number, the gig economy is having a significant impact on the labor market. Other countries that saw record low unemployment in the past few years tell a similar story. A 2016 study by McKinsey, also using a broad definition of independent work, finds that 36 percent of the working-age population in the UK are independent workers. The corresponding numbers are 25 percent in Germany, 28 percent in Sweden, and 31 percent in Spain.[17] France also has a high number of independent workers (30 percent) despite a stubbornly high unemployment rate, but that is mostly due to very rigid labor laws. In China, there is an estimated 110 million people active in the gig economy, working mainly as freelance writers, cab drivers, pet sitters, live streamers, or house cleaners, representing about 15 percent of the working-age population.[18]

There are many reasons why workers enter the gig economy. Those who do it by choice enjoy the independence, the flexible hours, being one's own boss, or not having to go through a lengthy hiring process. But there are others who simply do not have a choice, either because they are financially strapped or because they are unable to land a more traditional job (such as someone who has been laid off and works as an Uber driver whilst searching for their next job). The McKinsey study mentioned earlier points out that a majority of people (70 percent) become independent workers by choice, while the rest do so by necessity. Many observers are optimistic about this evolution, emphasizing the fact that independent workers often report higher levels of happiness with their work arrangements, at least for those who choose to be independent workers. They are free to choose when to work and what work to do, giving them more flexibility to manage their other life priorities.

But this is a short-term view. Although some in the gig economy, such as successful freelancers, make a very good living, most gig workers end up in low-paying jobs with little social safety, whether it relates to medical cover, pensions, paid leave, sick days, and minimum wage. The debate around whether to classify those workers as independent contractors or employees has generated many legal battles around the world. For most low-paid gig workers, social protection remains inadequate. It may not be much of a concern to them whilst they are in their twenties or thirties, but at some point, it will be. Workers in the gig economy could become a major burden to governments in a few decades when they retire with few savings and rising medical bills. Another issue is that most of those workers learn little during their various gig works: a person who works as an Uber driver during the first 10 or 15 years of his professional life will end up in his mid-thirties or early forties with little accumulated experience if that person ever needs to start another job.

Because most of those jobs are precarious with few learning opportunities, they contribute little to a country's productivity, the main driver of long-term growth. And because the majority of jobs created in the past decade are in the gig economy, they have done little to increase wages. We are not arguing that the unemployment rate has decreased in the past few years solely because of the emergence of the gig economy. Fewer people are unemployed because economies have picked up since the global financial crisis (before falling off a cliff in 2020). But without the gig economy, those unemployment numbers would not have fallen to historical lows.

For more than a century, the unemployment rate has been used as the main indicator to assess trends in the labor market. But with the rise of the gig economy, that indicator is in need of reinterpretation. It looks likely that in the years to come, policymakers will need to come up with new indicators that better reflect the state of the labor market. As Marion McGovern, author of a book on the gig economy, explains, "Our understanding of the cyclical nature of employment around business cycles may also shift, as workers secure additional work through digital platforms during downtimes, a practice that did not exist 30 years ago."[19] Central bankers in countries with record low unemployment rates need to be cognizant of these latest developments. Low unemployment figures are not necessarily a sign of an overheating economy or that current unemployment rates are below full employment rates. This should not be an automatic trigger to raise rates; doing so would merely prevent economies from reaching their full potential.

No Longer the Only Game in Town but Still Very Relevant

Monetary policy is a vast topic, certainly too vast to be covered extensively within a few pages. Other important matters for central banks include their role as lenders of last resort or their ability to identify and take corrective action against the emergence of 'bubbles' at times when asset prices no longer reflect the rational behavior of market participants. Much of the focus of this chapter has instead been on inflation and its relation to unemployment, topics that affect rich and poor countries alike.

The past decade has redefined monetary policy. Central banks around the world were thrown in the limelight and given the task of rescuing entire economies from total collapse, resorting to untested policies when the traditional tools at their disposal were no longer available, first during the 2008 subprime mortgage crisis, then during the 2010 European debt crisis, and now during the 2020 Covid-19 pandemic. They embraced their new responsibilities and responded admirably, injecting liquidity into economies in desperate need of it. Fiscal policy has played an important role as well, with large spending programs put in place by those nations most affected by the crises. Yet, any fiscal policy, however quickly it is announced, inevitably contains a time lag until it can be implemented and its effects deployed. By contrast, an overnight change in short-term interest rates or the large-scale purchase of financial assets have immediate consequences, affecting, among other things, the cost of borrowing and the value of various assets.

There are, however, time lags associated with monetary policy as well. This is the case when money does not flow through the economy. If banks are unwilling to lend, businesses unwilling to invest, and consumers unwilling to spend, economic recovery will be jeopardized. Growth was anemic for many years after the crises. This was not a result of any permanent changes in lending, investment, or consumption patterns; rather, it reflected a lack of confidence by people who had gone through the most traumatic financial crisis in living memory.

What monetary policy cannot do is rectify global imbalances whereby high-savings nations export their excess savings over investments at home to others that should be saving more. As indicated in the previous chapter, these imbalances are here to stay.

Perhaps the greatest lesson from the financial crisis has been the need to regulate and supervise the financial industry and, more specifically, the banks. Whilst pre-crisis policies focused on the ability of individual banks to remain liquid and solvent, little attention had been given to the contagion risk that the entire sector could become unstable. So-called macro-prudential measures have been discussed at length in recent years and are gradually being implemented. Examples include a cap on the amount of lending relative to the value of an asset (such as mortgages that cannot exceed a certain portion of the property value) or limits on debt relative to income. Bank regulations are also applied with different levels of assiduity: while the regulation of banks in developed countries has definitely improved, poorer nations often lack a comprehensive framework to tackle systemic risks such as the growth of non-performing loans, whether these loans are officially categorized as such or not. As a result, systemic risks to the financial sector will remain higher in emerging markets.

A Valuable World

This book has explored how the combination of human values and policies affects the economic outcome of nations. The harder people work, the higher the growth potential. The willingness and ability to save determines, to a large extent, whether a country will grow through investments and exports. Trust represents a major factor in explaining wealth and income inequalities. Economies with highly risk-averse citizens will stall. Other human values such as family ties, honesty, humility, leadership, and organizational skills likely play some role as well. Whilst the exact contribution of each of these values cannot be ascertained, this book has focused on the ones believed to have the greatest impact on an economy.

Identifying these values also has strong implications on the effectiveness of policies. Too often, these implications are ignored. We may believe that the same policies apply everywhere and will yield the same results. They do not. Countries where people do not trust each other should not attempt to reduce inequalities by increasing taxes; the result will be more corruption, not lower inequalities. Pushing for more exports and investments in a society where citizens are eager to spend most of their income is unlikely to work. Attempts to stimulate consumption in a society where people are unwilling to take risks will yield disappointing results.

Among the various values and policies examined in this book, hard work and free markets are probably the most conducive to growth. We cannot think of any country with a population identified as *both* hard-working (East Asian, South Asian, or historically Protestant) and a market economy that has not prospered. Similarly, no country without *both* a market economy and a hard-working population has ever prospered for an extended period of time, except for those nations that have done a good job managing their large and valuable natural resources. But nations that rely almost exclusively on natural resources will struggle the day those resources become depleted or are no longer in high demand. Countries with the greatest growth potential are those endowed with human values that are conducive to growth but which have failed to implement the right policies. Out of them, North Korea stands as the prime example.

Global Roundup

In Asia, home to more than half of the world's population, North Korea has the potential to become a first-world country within a generation or two. North Koreans are hard-working, thrifty, and much better educated than is commonly believed.[1] With the right policies in place, production and exports would ramp up quickly. Forget about the rockets, get the sanctions removed, join the World Trade Organization (WTO), implement sorely-needed market reforms, experiment with free-trade zones, and seriously crack down on corruption. But do not get carried away with growth at the risk of generating runaway inflation. The country can rely on its Chinese ally as a model; all it needs to do is to emulate it.

Other countries of Confucian heritage should continue to experience strong growth, except for Japan unless it manages to emerge from its current paralysis, a result of its inability to take risks. Vietnam, which has made strong economic progress since it abandoned its planned economy and joined the WTO in 2007, will grow even faster if it can make its domestic market more competitive and manages to fight widespread corruption. Malaysia, Indonesia, Thailand, and the Philippines all have market economies, but their future growth is hampered by weaker work ethics and high levels of corruption, with little willingness or ability to fight it. Despite strong growth over the past decade, these nations will struggle to reach a level of development attained by the likes of South Korea, Japan, or Taiwan.

South Asian countries have made significant progress in the past 30 years as they abandoned their planned economic model. They have not, however, fully embraced markets and have lagged behind East Asia as a result. In particular, India's growth has been mostly supported by the rise of the services sector, which remains far less regulated than manufacturing, a sector shackled by a raft of rules and regulations that prevents companies from operating on a level playing field in a free and fair competitive market environment.

Elsewhere, historically Protestant nations in Northern Europe, North America, and Australasia should continue to do well as long as they maintain their pro-market policies. Nordic countries such as Sweden may suffer from a drop in social trust as they welcome migrants with a different set of values, with potential consequences to their famed model of high taxes and social distributions. This is, however, unlikely to happen: measures have been taken to limit the inflow of migrants who, after successfully integrating within their new society, should contribute positively to ageing societies, thus reducing the financial burden to the state.

Russia has struggled to make the switch from a planned economy to a market-driven one. Despite a population generally considered as hardworking and well-educated, the economy has been mismanaged for decades and remains heavily reliant on natural resources. Most industries are overly regulated and unproductive. Many technically bankrupt companies, in the steel sector and elsewhere, are kept alive artificially by the state. There is too little focus on innovation. Private companies cannot compete in a fair way when the rules are distorted and arbitrary. Corruption is endemic. Russia's brightest emigrate to greener pastures where their talents can be better recognized. International sanctions and a declining population are not helping. For the country to realize its potential, it needs to allow private companies to operate on a level playing field between themselves and against state-owned entities, and to seriously crack down on corruption. Eastern European nations have experienced spectacular growth, first as they emerged out of the Soviet bloc, and then by joining the European Single Market. Nevertheless, just like other historically

Catholic nations, they are unlikely to catch up to the likes of Germany, the Netherlands, or Great Britain.

Southern Europe is finally emerging from its debt crisis following the global financial crisis. Yet, further catching up with their Northern European neighbors, as they did under European integration in the 1970s and 1980s, looks unlikely. The various problems that have plagued their economies over the years, whether due to human values not conducive to growth or weak policies, are likely to remain. Governments will change, but the brightest youth of those countries will continue to find more opportunities outside their borders than within them.

The outlook is also gloomy for Latin America and Africa. The sad reality is that none of those countries is expected to ever become a truly developed one, whatever the policies put in place. Excluding economies that depend mostly on natural resources, the best they can hope for is what a country such as Chile has achieved, the most prosperous nation in Latin America and, not coincidentally, the one where a process of creative destruction and fair competition is most visible. Yet, for all its achievements, Chile's gross domestic product (GDP) per capita remains four times lower than the United States and three times lower than Germany. Latin American and African nations also suffer from low social trust and large informal sectors that have resulted in highly unequal societies. Higher taxes will do little to effectively fight inequalities; a better approach involves the use of conditional cash transfers. On a more positive note, young populations (especially in Africa) and strong family ties reduce pension and healthcare costs, an increasingly high burden for governments in many advanced economies.

The growth of the African continent has been the focus of intense scrutiny over the past decades. There has been no shortage of theories to explain why Africa has lagged behind. As discussed earlier, although most Africans were born long after slavery was abolished, the slave trades played a vital role in shaping values and attitudes towards work, especially in those countries that were the most affected by it. The legacy of another historical factor — a colonial past — is less clear: if a colonial past was really an obstacle to growth, Singapore would still be a port town today and Liberia, which was never colonized, would not be one of the poorest countries in the world.

Other popular, more upbeat theories focus on aid, foreign lending, geography, or the rise of institutions, offering solutions that would supposedly propel many African nations to historical heights. But if there really were a miracle cure, would we not have figured it out by now? Africa comprises 54 countries, with very different policies, governments, ethnic groups, climates, and access to the sea. None of these countries (except for tiny Seychelles) is in the top 50 nations in the world with the highest GDP per capita, with most of them languishing at the bottom of that list. Why did none of them become another Sweden or Germany? This is not a statistical anomaly. The reason why the continent as a whole has struggled, and will continue to struggle, is a lack of human values conducive to growth, primarily a strong work ethic, something that has been acknowledged by some African leaders. Former Mozambique President Armando Guebuza once railed against "the lack of a habit of hard work [that] is perpetuating hunger and poverty" and the "massive apathy toward work in the country".[2] Botswana is an example of a country that has grown spectacularly in the 20th century since acquiring independence as a result of its ability to capitalize on abundant natural resources as well as the leadership of Seretse Khama, but which has more recently become stuck as a middle-income nation because of a lack of productivity, to a large extent caused by poor work ethics. In a recent global survey by the World Economic Forum, the main obstacle encountered by companies doing business in Botswana was the poor work ethics of local workers, more so than access to financing or weak infrastructure. In fact, Botswana took the unenviable top spot out of 137 countries in terms of poor work ethics.[3] In 2015, a local university professor lamented the population's work ethic and its direct impact on "the country's low volume of foreign direct investments. So common and accepted is the African time syndrome among the Batswana that a saying that 'There is no hurry in Botswana' has long taken root."[4] A study focusing on Chinese-owned shops in Gaborone looked at how different perceptions of work ethics have led to Chinese owners complaining about local assistants not working hard enough and assistants accusing shop owners of exploiting them.[5] When Quett Masire, who succeeded Seretse Khama as President, visited a shirt factory in Singapore in the 1980s, he observed that by the time the Botswana worker had produced one shirt, the

Singaporean worker had already produced six. This was not because of superior technology; it came down to the simple fact that the Singaporean worker was more hard-working. Masire would later comment, "This was productivity not in theory but in demonstrable terms. When we say we are not productive, this is what we meant." Masire attributed the low work ethic of his compatriots to the century-old tradition of raising cattle. As he put it, "Most of the time pastoralists are just lazing about as their cattle graze untended in the bush."[6] This is a far cry from Chinese workers laboring in paddy fields. Masire took matters in his own hands by establishing the Botswana National Productivity Centre in 1995, benchmarking it against Singapore and requesting the help of the Singapore government in implementing various initiatives to improve productivity. Unfortunately, these and subsequent efforts did not yield much result. Attitudes towards hard work or any other human value can seldom be changed. Labor productivity in Botswana has remained stagnant since the 1990s.[7]

That is not say that Africa cannot grow. In fact, many African nations have grown spectacularly in the past three decades. Armed conflicts are on the decline. Life expectancy, primary and secondary school enrollment, vaccination levels, and access to electricity have all improved significantly. Although westerners are loath to acknowledge it, China has played an important role, investing in the continent at a time when western financiers were pulling out. The Chinese model of building infrastructure without meddling into domestic affairs has been successful for both sides. Countries that have performed best are the ones with large natural resources that have been well-managed (Gabon and Botswana), but others less reliant on commodities have also done relatively well, such as Ethiopia, Rwanda, and Ghana.

A Growth Curve for Each Nation

Are we over-generalizing? Can we really summarize the long-term prospects of a nation in a few sentences? Perhaps we are over-generalizing, but we remain convinced that human values play a crucial role and should form the starting point to assess the growth potential of any economy.

Standard economic growth theory states that each country goes through a series of development stages along a growth curve. The assumption is that every country uses the same growth curve and that poor countries eventually catch up to the richer ones if they implement the right policies. But the reality is that each country has its own growth curve, largely shaped by the human values that characterize its population. Because values seldom change over time, different growth curves remain, implying different growth potentials. The corollary to this is that poor countries without human values conducive to growth can certainly grow, but they will never grow beyond a certain stage (again, unless they own valuable natural resources and are able to make the most of those resources).

Many emerging countries have become stuck in a middle-income trap. Their economies grow to a certain stage, but are unable to progress further. Brazil and South Africa are commonly cited as examples. Rising wages that make exports less competitive are often seen as the reason why those countries become 'stuck'. But if that were true, Taiwan, South Korea, or Singapore should also have gotten stuck in a middle-income trap. The reason some countries are unable to progress further is because they are reaching the top end of their own growth curve. Most Latin American and African countries have fallen, or are likely to fall, into such a trap. But East Asian, South Asian, and historically Protestant nations, at least those that have not yet reached the status of a modern economy, should avoid it. As Lee Kuan Yew once argued, "If you have a culture that doesn't place much value in learning and scholarship and hard work and thrift and deferment of present enjoyment for future gain, the going will be much slower."[8]

A Crisis Like no Other

As we write these lines in the summer of 2020, the world remains engulfed in the Covid-19 pandemic which has claimed the lives of hundreds of thousands of victims and affected the livelihood of millions. Many have lost their jobs and are unable to find a new one. Some struggle with basic necessities such as food, medicine, and shelter, especially in lower income countries.

This pandemic has profoundly altered the way we live and the way companies conduct their businesses. Lockdowns imposed in most countries have forced us to adapt to a very different reality. E-commerce has surged. Businesses and public administrations are accelerating the digitalization of their processes. Physical documents are switching to electronic form. Telecommuting has become the norm for many workers. Work from home is not always possible or as efficient. But overall, companies have realized that many functions that were previously thought to require a physical presence could be handled just as well remotely. The Covid-19 pandemic has challenged our natural tendency to resist change. As economic activity returns, some changes are likely to become permanent. Someone working at home on the outskirts of London or New York could just as well be working from Bangalore, Dalian, or Warsaw. Equipping workers with valuable and upgraded skills to navigate a globalized and changing world is becoming ever more critical.

The pandemic has also provided another reminder that the same policies can yield very different results in different places. We discussed in this book how countries with high levels of social trust have had much greater success in fighting the virus because people who generally trust each other are more likely to behave in a way that considers the interests of others and to follow the recommendations of their authorities. Epidemiologists, political scientists, sociologists, economists, and experts from other fields should consider how different people around the world often behave very differently. They should also talk to each other: a multidisciplinary approach can only improve our understanding of the best ways to fight this pandemic.

Covid-19 has severely restricted the ability of people to travel internationally and to interact with one another. The decline in conflicts observed since World War II is in no small part the result of people coming together, exchanging views, and resolving matters before they escalate. The more we interact with people of different nationalities, and also of different income levels, cultures, and ethnic backgrounds, the more we can understand them and enrich ourselves through that process. As national borders remain mostly shut, the risk is that those of us unable (or unwilling) to experience the world may cling onto misconceptions as to what motivates others to behave in a certain way. At a time of rising geopolitical tensions, a willingness to listen to others and to exchange ideas at every level of society remains the best way of moving forward.

A Valuable World

We began this book by briefly describing the lives of a few individuals scattered across the globe: Anja in Sweden who wondered whether others could still be trusted, Karabo the shop assistant, and her Chinese manager Mrs. Chen in Botswana. We described how the different values they grow up with guides their behavior. People around the world may have different values and come from different backgrounds, but they also have a lot in common. They are all part of the same world. They all aspire to a good life, even though that means different things to each of them. They may not realize it, but a brighter future is much more likely with economic growth, for it is growth that creates wealth and jobs and enables higher wages, a more educated workforce, better healthcare, and comfortable pensions. It is up to their leaders to implement the right policies, taking into account the human values that define the society they live in, to ensure that their people have a better chance of reaching their goals in life, and truly believe that the world they live in is a valuable one.

Endnotes

Prologue

1. The story is inspired by Zi Yanyin, *Iron Sharpens Iron: Social Interactions at China Shops in Botswana*, 2017; Zi Yanyin and Mogalakwe Monageng, *Decoding Relationships between Chinese Merchants and Batswana Shop Assistants: The Case of China Shops in Gaborone*, 2018

Introduction

1. Glenn Hubbard and Tim Kane, *Balance: The Economics of Great Powers from Ancient Rome to Modern America*, 2013.
2. Justin Yifu Lin, *The Quest for Prosperity: How Developing Economies Can Take Off*, 2013.
3. Joseph Henrich, Steven Heine, and Ara Norenzayan, *The weirdest people in the world?*, 2010.
4. Paul Collier, *The Bottom Billion: Why the Poorest Countries are Failing and What Can Be Done About It*, 2007.
5. Anthony Randazzo and Jonathan Haidt, *The Moral Narratives of Economists*, 2015.
6. Martin Ford, *Rise of the Robots: Technology and the Threat of a Jobless Future*, 2015.

Chapter 1

1. Robert J. Smith, *The Ethnic Japanese in Brazil*, 1979.
2. Matinas Suzuki Jr, *História da discriminação brasileira contra os japoneses sai do limbo in Folha de S. Paulo*, 2008 [in Portuguese].
3. Thomas H. Holloway, *Immigrants on the Land: Coffee and Society in São Paulo, 1886–1934*, 1980.
4. All coffee crops in the early 20th century were picked by hand. More recently, mechanized harvesting methods have been introduced, including in Brazil.
5. Ayumi Takenaka, *The Japanese in Peru: History of Immigration, Settlement, and Racialization*, 2004.
6. Donald Hastings, *Japanese Emigration and Assimilation in Brazil*, 1969; Robert J. Smith, *The Ethnic Japanese in Brazil*, 1979.
7. Jeffrey Lesser, *Negotiating National Identity: Migrants, Minorities, and the Struggle for Ethnicity in Brazil*, 1999.
8. Ibid.
9. Stewart Lone, *The Japanese Community in Brazil, 1908–1940: Between Samurai and Carnival*, 2001.
10. The data comes from Carlos Gradín, *Race and income distribution: Evidence from the US, Brazil and South Africa*, 2010 and was retrieved from the Brazilian National Household Survey in 2007. There is no distinction between Asians minorities, only an 'Asian' minority. Given that Japanese Brazilians represent the overwhelming majority of Asians in Brazil (around 80 percent according to the Brazilian Institute of Geography and Statistics, IBGE), we assume here that data on the Asian minority applies to the Japanese minority.
11. Gary Okihiro, *The Columbia Guide to Asian American History*, 2005.
12. Thomas Sowell, *Ethnic America*, 1981.
13. *Median Household Income in the Past 12 Months (in 2016 inflation-adjusted dollars)*, American Community Survey, 2016.
14. Eve Kushner, *Japanese-Peruvians Reviled and Respected: The Paradoxical Place of Peru's Nikkei*, 2007.
15. Ayumi Takenaka, *The Japanese in Peru: History of Immigration, Settlement, and Racialization*, 2004.
16. Alberto Fujimori was convicted of bribery and human rights violations. He has been jailed since 2009.
17. Oxford dictionary.
18. *Alexei Stakhanov: The USSR's superstar miner*, BBC Magazine, December 30, 2015.

19. We should bear in mind that there are various complications when applying these individual measures to an entire country and making international comparisons, including total hours worked versus total paid hours worked, full-time work versus full-time and part-time, and real exchange rates versus purchasing power parity.

20. The Conference Board Total Economy Database, 2018.

21. *Alexei Stakhanov: The USSR's superstar miner*, BBC Magazine, December 30, 2015.

22. World Values Survey Wave 6: 2010–2014.

23. Gordon Redding, *The Spirit of Chinese Capitalism*, 1993.

24. CIA World Factbook.

25. Gordon Redding, *The Spirit of Chinese Capitalism*, 1993 contains economic data on the Chinese community in various Southeast Asian countries in terms of market capitalization, privately-owned companies, and wealthiest individuals.

26. There are, unfortunately, few statistics available of ethnic Chinese population by province for countries in which the Chinese represent a significant portion of the overall population. In Southeast Asia, only Malaysia provides such data.

27. Gross domestic product per capita for each state is from the Department of Statistics Malaysia, State Socioeconomic Report 2018. The ethnic Chinese population by state is extracted from the 2010 Census (Malaysia performs a census every 10 years).

28. In 2016, American households of Chinese origin had a median income of $84,764, compared to $57,617 of United States median household income that same year (source: American Community Survey, United States Census Bureau).

29. *For Asians, School Tests Are Vital Steppingstones*, New York Times, October 26, 2012.

30. Median Household Income in the Past 12 Months, American Community Survey, United States Census Bureau, 2016.

31. CIA World Factbook.

32. See, for example, Min Zhan, *Assets, parental expectations and involvement, and children's educational performance*, 2005.

33. Herman Kahn, *World Economic Development: 1979 and Beyond*, 1979.

34. Arthur Henderson Smith, *Chinese Characteristics*, 1890.

35. Abraham Lu, William Dowell, and Winter Nie, *In the Shadow of the Dragon: The Global Expansion of Chinese Companies — and How It Will Change Business Forever*, 2012.

36. Quoted in John and Doris Naisbitt, *China's Megatrends: The 8 Pillars of a New Society*, 2010.
37. William H. Overholt, *China's Crisis of Success*, 2018.
38. Judith Djamour, *Malay Kinship and Marriage in Singapore*, 1959, quoted from Fook Kwang Han, Warren Fernandez, and Sumiko Tan, *Lee Kuan Yew, The Man and His Ideas*, 1998.
39. *A Conversation with Lee Kuan Yew*, Fareed Zakaria, 1994.
40. GDP per capita, current USD, the World Bank, 2019.
41. Angus Maddison, *The World Economy: Historical Statistics*, 2003; Cristobal Young, *Religion and Economic Growth in Western Europe: 1500–2000*, 2009.
42. Calvinists did believe in predestination, the idea that our fate is sealed, whatever our actions. But they also believed that certain signs could give an indication of whether someone was predestined for Heaven, such as a materialistically successful life.
43. See, for example, Sascha O. Becker and Ludger Wößmann, *Was Weber Wrong? A Human Capital Theory of Protestant Economic History*, 2007.
44. Nathan Nunn, *The Long-Term Effects of Africa's Slave Trades*, 2008.
45. Thomas Sowell, *The Economics and Politics of Race: An International Perspective*, 1983.
46. Quoted in Lawrence E. Harrison, *Who Prospers: How Cultural Values Shape Economic and Political Success*, 1992.

Chapter 2

1. *Those frugal Germans*, Deutsche Welle, November 26, 2012.
2. *Why are Germans so obsessed with saving money?*, Financial Times, March 22, 2018.
3. Ibid.
4. John Knowles and Andrew Postlewaite, *Do Children Learn to Save From Their Parents?*, 2004.
5. A more complete definition of household savings is disposable income less consumption, adjusted for the change in pension entitlement.
6. Luigi Guiso, Paola Sapienza, and Luigi Zingales, *Does Culture Affect Economic Outcomes?*, 2006.
7. Christopher D. Carroll, Byung-Kun Rhee, and Changyong Rhee , *Are There Cultural Effects on Saving? Some Cross-Sectional Evidence*, 1994.

8. Christopher D. Carroll, Byung-Kun Rhee, and Changyong Rhee, *Does Cultural Origin Affect Saving Behavior? Evidence from Immigrants*, 1998. The figure of 92 percent born in the United States is from the 1990 Census.

9. Paolo Masella, Hannah Paule-Paludkiewicz, and Nicola Fuchs-Schündeln, *Cultural Determinants of Household Saving Behavior*, 2017.

10. This could also be related to income levels or the number of children: migrants to Germany usually have lower incomes compared to German households and their children are more likely to end up with a lower income as well. Since low-income households save less, this may be more the result of income correlation between generations rather than due to how people value thrift. Migrants also tend to have more children, which could reduce their savings because of additional spending, and also because of the expectation that their children will financially support them in old age. But even after taking into consideration income levels, the number of children, and education level, among other factors, the savings rates of second-generation migrants remained similar to the ones of their country of origin.

11. Joan Costa-Font, Paola Giuliano, and Berkay Ozcan, *The Cultural Origin of Saving Behavior*, 2018.

12. Gross savings differ from net savings, which take into account asset depreciation. Net savings would appear to be the better indicator, but given the difficulty in estimating accurate depreciation values and the fact that data on gross savings rates is more readily available for most countries, throughout this chapter and this book we focus on gross savings rates.

13. Throughout the chapter, we consider that consumption includes government spending.

14. CIA World Factbook.

15. All national savings rates mentioned in this book are gross savings from the World Bank national accounts data and OECD National Accounts data files. Some of the rates are from 2017.

16. Mei Wang, Marc Oliver Rieger, and Thorsten Hens, *How Time Preferences Differ: Evidence from 45 Countries*, 2011.

17. Thrift does not fully explain these results. It could be that those with low incomes may not be able to afford to wait an additional month for that extra income. Another factor is trust: people in countries where trust is in short supply may have viewed this situation as a case of a smaller but certain amount of cash now versus a higher but less certain amount a month later.

18. Taha Choukhmane, Nicholas Coeurdacier, and Keyu Jin, *The One-Child Policy and Household Savings*, 2014.
19. Khaled A. Hussein and A. P. Thirlwall, *Explaining Differences in the Domestic Savings Ratio Across Countries: A Panel Data Study*, 1999.
20. Stefan Arendt and Wolfgang Nagl, *Unemployment Benefit and Wages: The Impact of the Labor Market Reform in Germany on (Reservation) Wages*, 2011.
21. CIA World Factbook, 2017 figures.
22. Fortune Magazine, November 2003 Issue.
23. Household savings, OECD Data, 2017.
24. Masahiko Nakazawa, Kazuaki Kikuta, and Yasutaka Yoneta, *The Saving Behavior of Elderly People in Japan: Analysis Based on Micro-Data from the National Survey of Family Income and Expenditure*, 2018.
25. Chadwick C. Curtis, Steven Lugauer, and Nelson C. Mark, *Demographics and Aggregate Household Saving in Japan, China, and India*, 2015.
26. John Maynard Keynes, *Essays in Persuasion*, 1930.
27. George Akerlof and Robert J. Shiller, *Phishing for Phools: The Economics of Manipulation and Deception*, 2015.
28. Ibid.
29. *Four dresses and a drone — are weddings getting out of control?*, BBC News, April 26, 2017.
30. National Financial Capability Study, FINRA, 2015.
31. Dean Karlan, Sendhil Mullainathan, and Benjamin N. Roth, *Debt Traps? Market Vendors and Moneylender Debt in India and the Philippines*, 2018.
32. Martin Rein and John Turner, *Public-Private Interactions: Mandatory Pensions in Australia, the Netherlands and Switzerland*, 2001.
33. Niall Ferguson, *The Ascent of Money: A Financial History of the World*, 2009.
34. Brigitte Madrian and Dennis Shea, *The Power of Suggestion: Inertia in 401(k) Participation and Savings Behavior*, 2001.
35. Global Findex database 2017, World Bank.
36. *Boosting domestic savings in Africa*, Africa Renewal (United Nations publication), October 2008.
37. *More People In The Developing World Are Getting Bank Accounts, But There's An Asterisk On That Progress*, The Huffington Post, April 15, 2015.
38. Global Findex database 2017, World Bank.
39. *Mobile financial services in Africa: Winning the battle for the customer*, September 2017, McKinsey & Company.
40. Abhijit V. Banerjee and Esther Duflo, *Poor Economics*, 2011.

Chapter 3

1. *SA court rules lockdown restrictions 'irrational'*, BBC News, June 3, 2020.
2. Sweden is an interesting case. It recorded fewer cases and deaths per capita compared to the likes of the United Kingdom, France, Italy, or Spain, but many more compared to other Nordic countries despite high levels of trust in others. This is often attributed to the absence of a lockdown, which probably did play a role. But another important factor is the large foreign population in Sweden where trust levels in others are much lower. Most infections occurred in migrant neighborhoods and most deaths were in elderly care homes, where visits were banned. The only way the virus could have spread in elderly care homes is through nurses and other staff, which in elderly care homes is disproportionally made up of migrant workers: according to the National Board of Health and Welfare, 28 percent of healthcare workers in elderly care homes are non-Swedish, rising to 55 percent in Stockholm. The majority of migrants originate from war-torn countries where trust in others is understandably much lower. They live in larger families, often do manual work that cannot be done from home (bus or taxi drivers, cleaning services, or security guards), may not have a good understanding of the Swedish language, and may have an oral tradition that favors receiving oral information from a known source over written communications.
3. See Steven F. Messner, Richard Rosenfeld, and Eric P. Baumer, *Dimensions of Social Capital and Rates of Criminal Homicide*, 2004 for the link between social trust and the crime rate in the United States. On the relation between social trust and happiness, see John F. Helliwell, Haifung Huang, and Shun Wang, *New Evidence on Trust and Well-being*, 2016. See also Yausharu Tokuda, Seiji Fujii, and Takashi Inoguchi, *Individual and Country-Level Effects of Social Trust on Happiness: The Asia Barometer Survey*, 2010 based on a study of 29 Asian countries.
4. Joyce Berg, John Dickhaut, and Kevin McCabe, *Trust, Reciprocity, and Social History*, 1995.
5. Edward Glaeser, David Laibson, Jose Scheinkman, and Christine Soutter, *Measuring trust*, 2000.
6. Among others: the Afrobarometer in Africa, the European Social Survey, the China General Social Survey, the General Social Survey in the United States, the Asian and East Asia Barometers, and Latinobarometro in Latin America.
7. Ryan E. Carlin, Gregory J. Love, and Conal Smith, *Measures of interpersonal trust: Evidence on their cross-national validity and reliability based on surveys and experimental data*, 2017.

8. The only country that comes close to Sweden is China, but as we have discussed in an earlier chapter, when asked the question of whether they generally trust others, many Chinese respondents believe that the question relates to people they already know.

9. European Social Survey, Round 8 (2016).

10. Richard Traunmüller, *Moral Communities? Religion as a Source of Social Trust in a Multilevel Analysis of 97 German Regions*, 2011.

11. T. F. G Brinkman, *Religion and Social trust in the Netherlands*, 2014; Maryam Dilmaghani, *Religiosity and social trust: evidence from Canada*, 2016.

12. *Americans and Social Trust: Who, Where and Why*, 2006, Pew Research Center.

13. Lars Torpe and Henrik Lolle, *Identifying Social Trust in Cross-Country Analysis: Do We Really Measure the Same?*, 2011.

14. Confederation of Industry survey, 2011.

15. Eric M. Uslaner, *Where You Stand Depends upon Where Your Grandparents Sat: The Inheritability of Generalized Trust*, 2008. See also Robert D. Putnam, *Bowling Alone: The Collapse and Revival of American Community*, 2000.

16. Yann Algan and Pierre Cahuc, *Inherited Trust and Growth*, 2010.

17. Thomas Cusack, *On the road to Weimar? The political economy of popular satisfaction with government and regime performance*, 1997.

18. World Values Survey Wave 6, 2010–2014.

19. Alberto Alesina and Eliana La Ferrara, *Who trusts others?*, 2002.

20. See, for example, Paul J. Zak and Stephen Knack, *Trust and Growth*, 2001.

21. Stephen Knack, *Social Capital and the Quality of Government: Evidence from the States*, 2002.

22. General Social Survey; Thomas Piketty, *Capital in the Twenty-First Century*, 2013.

23. *Long-Term International Migration into and out of the UK by citizenship, 1964 to 2015*, Office for National Statistics, 2016. It would have been useful to observe social trust in London compared to other cities or regions in the United Kingdom since most migrants settled in London, but unfortunately such data is unavailable.

24. Data on social trust among various communities in the United States is surprisingly difficult to find. The General Social Survey does not consider Hispanics as a race, but as an ethnic group; as such it incorporates them into White and Black categories. The Pew Research Center does provide a distinction between Whites, Blacks, and Hispanics. Data from the United Kingdom is even more limited as survey respondents on social

trust are not categorized according to their ethnic group. We have compared the ethnic diversity of the United Kingdom population between 1990 and 1999 and assigned a social trust percentage to minorities based on their country of origin to derive a national weighted average.

25. Robert Putnam, *E Pluribus Unum: Diversity and Community in the Twenty-first Century*, 2007; Maurice Gesthuizen, Tom Van Der Meer, and Peer Scheepers, *Ethnic Diversity and Social Capital in Europe*, 2009. A large part of the discussion focuses on the concept of social capital, which, apart from social trust, often includes participation in voluntary organizations, meeting with various social groups, and donations. See also Debby Gerritsen and Marcel Lubbers, *Unknown is unloved? Diversity and inter-population trust in Europe*, 2010 for a discussion on the impact of cultural distance on social trust in Europe.

26. Alberto Alesina and Eliana La Ferrara, *Who trusts others?*, 2002.

27. Sweden Statistics (SCB).

28. *The shifting sands of Sweden's immigration debate*, The Local SE, June 26, 2018.

29. *Seeking asylum — and jobs*, The Economist, November 5, 2016.

30. *Northern lights*, The Economist, February 2, 2013.

31. See, for example, Magnus Carlsson and Dan-Olof Rooth, *Evidence of ethnic discrimination in the Swedish labor market using experimental data*, 2006.

32. *In Sweden, Riots Put an Identity in Question,* New York Times, May 26, 2013.

33. Karl McShane, *Getting used to diversity? Immigration and trust in Sweden*, 2017.

Chapter 4

1. Charles A. Holt and Susan K. Laury, *Risk Aversion and Incentive Effects*, 2002.

2. World Values Survey Wave 6: 2010–2014, V76. The actual question is whether respondents identify with a person who is adventurous and takes risks. The two negative answers ('Not like me' and 'Not at all like me') are grouped together to describe risk-averse persons.

3. Armin Falk, Anke Becker, Thomas Dohmen, Benjamin Enke, David Huffman, and Uwe Sunde , *Global Evidence on Economic Preferences*, 2018.

4. World Values Survey Wave 6 and 2018 GDP per capita in current US$ as per the World Bank. The correlation coefficient comes out to 0.22.

5. Luigi Guiso, Paola Sapienza, and Luigi Zingales, *Time Varying Risk Aversion*, 2018.

6. Yihui Pan, Stephan Siegel, and Tracy Yue Wang, *The Cultural Origin of Preferences: CEO Cultural Heritage and Corporate Investment*, 2014.

7. See Holger Bonin, Amelie Constant, Konstantinos Tatsiramos, and Klaus F. Zimmermann, *Native-Migrant Differences in Risk Attitudes*, 2006 for a review of German first and second-generation migrants and their attitudes towards risk.

8. For an overview see Christoph S. Weber, *Cultural Differences in Risk Tolerance*, 2013.

9. Jaimie Sung and Sherman D. Hanna, *Factors Related to Risk Tolerance*, 1997.

10. See, for example, Catia Batista and Janis Umblijs, *Migration, Risk Attitudes, and Entrepreneurship: Evidence from a Representative Immigrant Survey*, 2014.

11. Areendam Chanda and Bulent Unel, *Do Attitudes toward Risk Taking Affect Entrepreneurship? Evidence from Second-Generation Americans*, 2019.

12. Investment share of purchasing power parity converted GDP per capita at constant prices for Japan (Source: Federal Reserve Bank of St. Louis).

13. *Japan Inc. sitting on ¥506.4 trillion mountain of cash*, The Japan Times, September 3, 2019. Investment, or gross capital formation, represented 25 percent of GDP in 2018 according to the Ministry of Finance.

14. *Risk On*, The Economist, March 15, 2014.

15. OECD Factbook, 2015–2016.

16. *Back to reality*, EY global venture capital trends 2015.

17. Doing Business, The World Bank, June 2017. See also Clyde Prestowitz, *Japan Restored: How Japan Can Reinvent Itself and Why This Is Important for America and the World*, 2015.

18. Global Entrepreneurship Monitor 2017/2018.

19. *Japan's chance to replicate Silicon Valley dogged by risk aversion: Abe*, Bloomberg, May 2, 2015.

20. Tomoko Namba, quoted in Brian Salsberg, Clay Chandler, and Heang Chhor, *Reimagining Japan: The Quest for a Future that Works*, 2011.

21. Clyde Prestowitz, *Japan Restored: How Japan Can Reinvent Itself and Why This Is Important for America and the World*, 2015.

22. Ulrike Malmendier and Stefan Nagel, *Learning from Inflation Experiences*, 2016. See also Ulrike Malmendier and Stefan Nagel, *Depression Babies: Do Macroeconomic Experiences Affect Risk Taking?*, 2011.

23. The Annual Report on European SMEs, 2017–2018.
24. *The future of SME banking: Minds made for redefining financial services*, Ernst & Young, December 2018.
25. *SMEs in Europe lack an estimated 400bn of bank-financing*, Euler Hermes study, April 2019.
26. *SME financing in the euro area*, Deutsche Bank Research, 2014.
27. *Return on Average Equity for all U.S. Banks*, Federal Reserve Bank of St. Louis.
28. *Return on equity in Nordic banking sector 2011–2016*, Bank of Finland Bulletin; *The profitability of banks in a context of negative monetary policy rates: the cases of Sweden and Denmark*, European Central Bank, August 2017.
29. *Global Bank Job Cull Tops 75,000 This Year as UniCredit Cuts*, Bloomberg News, December 3, 2019.

Chapter 5

1. Jonathan Power, *Ending War Crimes, Chasing the War Criminals*, 2017.
2. Robert J. Barro, *Democracy & Growth*, 1994.
3. See, for example, Dani Rorik and Romain Wacziarg, *Do Democratic Transitions Produce Bad Economic Outcomes?*, 2005 or, more recently, Daron Acemoglu, Suresh Naidu, Pascual Restrepo, and James A. Robinson, *Democracy Does Cause Growth*, 2016.
4. Ari Aisen and Francisco Jose Veiga, *How Does Political Instability Affect Economic Growth?*, 2011. See also Alberto Alesina, Sule Ozler, Nouriel Roubini, and Phillip Swagel, *Political instability and economic growth*, 1996; Richard Jong-A-Pin, *On the Measurement of Political Stability and its Impact on Economic Growth*, 2009.
5. Paul Collier and Nicholas Sambanis, *Understanding Civil War*, 2002.
6. Paul Collier and Anke Hoeffler, *Murder by Numbers: Socio-Economic Determinants of Homicide and Civil War*, 2004.
7. Edward Miguel, Sebastian M. Saiegh, and Shanker Satyanath, *Civil War Exposure and Violence*, 2011.
8. For an overview, see Michael Bleaney and Arcangelo Dimico, *Ethnic Diversity and Conflict*, 2016.
9. Paul Collier, *The Bottom Billion: Why the Poorest Countries are Failing and What Can Be Done About It*, 2007.
10. Nathan Nunn, Nancy Qian, and Jaya Wen, *Distrust and Political Turnover*, 2017.

Chapter 6

1. Alejandro Foxley, *Successes and Failures in Poverty Eradication: Chile*, 2004.
2. Michael Margitich, *The 1982 Debt Crisis and Recovery in Chile*, 1999; Ricardo Ffrench-Davis, *Is Chile a Role Model for Development*, 2015.
3. La Tribune, March 17, 2013 [in French].
4. *Zombie Hordes: Thousands of Japanese Firms Dodging Bankruptcy*, Bloomberg, March 13, 2017.
5. Ricardo J. Caballero, Takeo Hoshi, and Anil K. Kashyap, *Zombie Lending and Depressed Restructuring in Japan*, 2008.
6. *Japan aims to double service-sector productivity growth*, Nikkei Asian Review, March 4, 2016.
7. *Japan's top convenience stores dominate like never before*, Nikkei Asian Review, July 23, 2014.
8. Cheng Han Tan, Dan W. Puchniak, and Umakanth Varottil, *State-Owned Enterprises in Singapore: Historical Insights into a Potential Model for Reform*, 2015.
9. Carlos Ramirez and Ling Hui Tan, *Singapore, Inc. Versus the Private Sector: Are Government-Linked Companies Different?*, 2003.
10. Joseph Schumpeter, *Capitalism, Socialism and Democracy*, 1942.
11. See Joe Studwell, *How Asia Works: Success and Failure in the World's Most Dynamic Region*, 2014 for an excellent overview of how East Asian economies developed in the 20th century.
12. *Yearbook of Statistics Singapore, 2017.*
13. Guillaume Duteurtre, Mbène Dieye Faye, and Papa Nouhine Dieye, *L'agriculture sénégalaise à l'épreuve du marché*, 2010; François-Xavier Branthôme, *Sénégal: une filière en grande difficulté*, 2018 [in French].
14. International Food Policy Research Institute, *Substituting for rice imports in Ghana*, 2014.
15. Simeon Djankov, Caroline Freund, and Cong S. Pham, *Trading on Time*, 2010
16. *The rise and fall of Britain's steel industry*, BBC News, May 22, 2016.

Chapter 7

1. *Die Talentiertesten wollen Lehrer werden*, Süddeutsche Zeitung, December 27, 2010 [in German].

2. Hannu Simola, Jaakko Kauko, Janne Varjo, Mira Kalalahti, and Fritjof Sahlström, *Dynamics in Education Politics and the Finnish PISA Miracle*, 2017.

3. Hannu Simola, *The Finnish Education Mystery: Historical and Sociological Essays on Schooling in Finland*, 2015.

4. The petition can be found (in English) at: https://matematiikkalehtisolmu.fi/2005/erik/PisaEng.html.

5. Hannu Simola, *The Finnish miracle of PISA: Historical and sociological remarks on teaching and teacher education*, 2005.

6. *Lighting your way to a better future.* Speech delivered by Nelson Mandela at the launch of Mindset Network, July 16, 2003.

7. Amartya Sen, *Development as Freedom*, 1999.

8. UNESCO Institute for Statistics, 2017.

9. *Government expenditure on education, total (% of GDP)*, The World Bank, using data from the UNESCO Institute of Statistics.

10. *The US spends more on education than other countries. Why is it falling behind?*, The Guardian, September 7, 2018.

11. *Homework for all*, The Economist, December 10, 2016.

12. Education at a Glance, OECD, 2017.

13. Esther Duflo, Pascaline Dupas, and Michael Kremer, *School Governance, Teacher Incentives, and Pupil-Teacher Ratios: Experimental Evidence from Kenyan Primary Schools*, 2014.

14. *Tuition madness, Gangnam style*, TODAY, November 16, 2013.

15. *Parents in Spain go on homework strike*, BBC News, November 4, 2016.

16. Thomas L. Friedman, *The World is Flat: A Brief History of the Twenty-first Century*, 2006.

17. *Does homework perpetuate inequities in education?*, OECD, 2014.

18. Joshua D. Angrist, Parag A. Pathak, and Christopher R. Walters, *Explaining Charter School Effectiveness*, 2013; *KIPP's explosive growth came with slight dip in performance, study says*, Washington Post, September 17, 2015.

19. Raj Chetty, John N. Friedman, Nathaniel Hilger, Emmanuel Saez, Diane Whitmore Schanzenbach, and Danny Yagan, *How Does Your Kindergarten Classroom Affect Your Earnings? Evidence from Project STAR*, 2011.

20. See, for example, Susanna Loeb and Marianne E. Page, *Examining the Link Between Teacher Wages and Student Outcomes: The Importance of Alternative Labor Market Opportunities and Non-Pecuniary Variation*, 2000.

21. Ernesto Dal Bó, Frederico Finan, and Martín Rossi, *Strengthening State Capabilities: The Role of Financial Incentives in the Call to Public Service*, 2013.

22. 2013 Global Teacher Status Index, Varkey GEMS Foundation.

23. 2013 OECD Teaching and Learning International Survey.
24. Ibid.
25. *School teacher sets record for missing 23 of 24-year teaching career*, First-Post, August 25, 2014.
26. Nazmul Chaudhury, Jeffrey Hammer, Michael Kremer, Karthik Muralid-haran, and F. Halsey Rogers, *Missing in Action: Teacher and Health Worker Absence in Developing Countries*, 2006.
27. Esther Duflo, Rema Hanna, and Stephen P. Ryan, *Incentives Work: Getting Teachers to Come to School*, 2010.
28 *How many children are not in school?*, The World Bank, January 23, 2019.
29. *World Inequality Database in Education*, 2014 based on the *2010 Burundi Demographic and Health Survey.*
30. David Evans, Michael Kremer, and Muthoni Ngatia, *The Impact of Distributing School Uniforms on Children's Education in Kenya*, 2009.
31. Richard Dobbs, James Maniyka, and Jonathan Woetzel, *No Ordinary Disruption*, 2015.
32. Kyle Fee, Matt Klesta, and Lisa Nelson, *Addressing Employment Needs through Sector Partnerships: Case studies from across the Federal Reserve's Fourth District*, 2016.

Chapter 8

1. *Mobutu's Village Basks in His Glory*, New York Times, September 29, 1988; *Leaving Fire in His Wake*, Time Magazine, June 24, 2001; *Where Concorde once flew: The story of President Mobutu's 'African Versailles'*, The Guardian, February 10, 2015.
2. Robert I. Rotberg, *The Corruption Cure: How Citizens and Leaders Can Combat Graft*, 2017.
3. Bo Rothstein and Eric M. Uslaner, *All for All: Equality, Corruption and Social Trust*, 2006.
4. Raymond Fisman and Edward Miguel, *Cultures of Corruption: Evidence From Diplomatic Parking Tickets*, 2007.
5. *Kenyans have had it with corruption. Their leaders may finally be doing something about it*, Washington Post, July 17, 2018.
6. Robert I. Rotberg, *The Corruption Cure: How Citizens and Leaders Can Combat Graft*, 2017.
7. Paul Collier, *Growth Strategies for Africa*, 2007.
8. Transparency International Corruption Perceptions Index, 2019.

9. T. N. Ninan, *Turn of the Tortoise: The Challenge and Promise of India's Future*, 2017.
10. Ibid.
11 Ritva Reinikka and Jakob Svensson, *Fighting Corruption to Improve Schooling: Evidence from a Newspaper Campaign in Uganda*, 2005.
12. Business Insider India, August 28, 2013.
13. T. N. Ninan, *Turn of the Tortoise: The Challenge and Promise of India's Future*, 2017.

Chapter 9

1. The GINI index for Peru, which measures income inequality, went from 0.50 in 2005 to 0.43 in 2017 (source: Federal Reserve Bank of St. Louis). Nicola Anne Jones, Rosana Vargas, and Eliana Villar, *Cash Transfers to Tackle Childhood Poverty and Vulnerability: An Analysis of Peru's Juntos Programme*, 2008; Elizaveta Perova and Renos Vakis, *Welfare Impacts of the "Juntos" Program in Peru: Evidence From a Non-Experimental Evaluation*, 2009.
2. Sara J. Solnick and David Hemenway, *Is more always better?: A survey on positional concerns*, 1997.
3. Sumit Agarwal, Vyacheslav Mikhed, and Barry Scholnick, *Does the Relative Income of Peers Cause Financial Distress? Evidence from Lottery Winners and Neighboring Bankruptcies*, 2018.
4. Richard Easterlin, *The Economics of Happiness*, 2004.
5. Katherine A. DeCelles and Michael I. Norton, *Physical and situational inequality on airplanes predicts air rage*, 2016.
6. Mathias Trabandt and Harald Uhlig, *The Laffer curve revisited*, 2011; Alejandro Badel and Mark Huggett, *The sufficient statistic approach: Predicting the top of the Laffer curve*, 2017.
7. French Finance Ministry, 2015.
8. Kiridaran Kanagaretnam, Jimmy Lee, and Chee Yeow Lim, *Societal Trust and Corporate Tax Avoidance*, 2013.
9. The correlation comes from Henrik Jacobsen Kleven, *How Can Scandinavians Tax So Much?*, 2014 in which Figure 6 Panel A compares Tax/GDP ratio as the share of tax revenue in a given country's nominal GDP in 2012 (source: Index of Economic Freedom, Heritage Foundation) to the weighted-average survey response to the question of whether most people can be trusted, on a binary scale (source: World Values Survey).
10. World Values Survey, 2015.

11. Richard H. Thaler and Shlomo Benartzi, *Save More Tomorrow™: Using Behavioral Economics to Increase Employee Saving*, 2004.

12. By some accounts, Sub-Saharan Africa has also seen a slight decrease in income inequality. See, for example, Evridiki Tsounta and Anayochukwu I. Osueke, *What is Behind Latin America's Declining Income Inequality?*, 2014, International Monetary Fund Working Paper.

13. *Burden sharing*, The Economist, January 20, 2014.

14. *Latin America remains the most unequal region in the world*, OXFAM, December 19, 2017.

15. Marco Stampini and Leopoldo Tornarolli, *The Growth of Conditional Cash Transfers in Latin America and the Caribbean: Did They Go Too Far?*, 2012.

16. Sergei Soares, Rafael Osorio, Fabio Veras Soares, Marcelo Medeiros, and Eduardo Zepeda, *Conditional Cash Transfers in Brazil, Chile and Mexico: Impacts upon Inequality*, 2009.

17. Marco Stampini and Leopoldo Tornarolli, *The Growth of Conditional Cash Transfers in Latin America and the Caribbean: Did They Go Too Far?*, 2012.

Chapter 10

1. *A worthless currency*, The Economist, July 17, 2008.

2. *Who wants to be a trillionaire?*, The Economist, May 12, 2016.

3. *Zimbabwe to defer release of inflation figures, economy to contract in 2019 — finance minister*, Reuters, August 1, 2019.

4. Small nations with a limited domestic market often fix their currency to another (or a basket of other currencies). For example, Hong Kong pegs its currency to the US dollar. Singapore uses a weighted-average exchange rate and adjusts it within an undisclosed range. Botswana uses a crawling peg that focuses on the difference between the local inflation rate and the inflation rate of its main trading partners. All these nations require sizable foreign currency reserves to ensure the sustainability of their monetary policy.

5. Internal Reserves and Foreign Currency Liquidity, International Monetary Fund, January 2020.

6. See, for example, Eldar Shafir, Peter Diamond, and Amos Tversky, *Money Illusion*, 1997.

7. Robert J. Shiller, *Why Do People Dislike Inflation?*, 1997.

8. Stated differently, their expectation about future price increases moves above zero.

9. George A. Akerlof, William T. Dickens, and George L. Perry, *Near-Rational Wage and Price Setting and the Long-Run Phillips Curve*, 2000.

10. David G. Blanchflower, *Not Working: Where Have All the Good Jobs Gone?*, 2019.

11. The numbers quoted for Lyft, Didi Chuxing, Airbnb, and Grubhub are available on their website; *'I made $3.75 an hour': Lyft and Uber drivers push to unionize for better pay*, The Guardian, March 22, 2019. The number of Airbnb hosts is not disclosed, only the number of listings; one host can have multiple listings.

12. According to the Bureau of Labor Statistics, as of June 2019, there were 9.1 million unemployed persons for an unemployment rate of 3.7 percent.

13. Lawrence F. Katz and Alan B. Krueger, *The Rise and Nature of Alternative Work Arrangements in the United States, 1995–2015*, 2016.

14. Shane McFeely and Ryan Pendell, *What Workplace Leaders Can Learn From the Real Gig Economy*, 2018.

15. *Report on the Economic Well-Being of U.S. Households in 2017*, Federal Reserve, May 2018.

16. *Contingent and Alternative Employment Arrangements Summary*, Bureau of Labor Statistics, June 2018.

17. *Independent Work, Choice, Necessity, and the Gig Economy*, McKinsey Global Institute, October 2016.

18. *Labor force in China from 2006 to 2016*, Statista, October 2017.

19. Marion McGovern, *Thriving in the Gig Economy: How to Capitalize and Compete in the New World of Work*, 2017.

A Valuable World

1. In *A Capitalist in North Korea: My Seven Years in the Hermit Kingdom* (2014), Swiss entrepreneur Felix Abt describes his seven years working in North Korea. An educated workforce is seen as key to the survival of the nation. Aside from nationalism and ideology, mathematics, science, and languages feature prominently in school curriculums. North Korea would not be launching nuclear missiles or hacking into foreign mainframe computers without a highly educated elite.

2. *How Africa is Creating Welfare States*, The Economist, February 23, 2019.

3. *2017–2018 Global Competitiveness Report*, World Economic Forum.

4. Christian John Makgala, *There is no hurry in Botswana: Scholarship and stereotypes on "African time" syndrome in Botswana, 1895–2011*, 2015.

5. Yanyin Zi and Monageng Mogalakwe, *Decoding Relationships Between Chinese Merchants and Batswana Shop Assistants: the Case of China Shops in Gaborone*, 2018.

6. *Batswana have the worst work ethic in the world*, Sunday Standard, October 20, 2017.

7. *Total Factor Productivity at Constant National Prices for Botswana*, Federal Reserve Bank of St Louis, 1989–2014.

8. *A Conversation with Lee Kuan Yew*, Fareed Zakaria, 1994.

About the Authors

ChinHwee Tan is the Asia-Pacific CEO of a global Fortune 25 company and was previously the founding Asia partner of the top 3 largest alternatives investors in the world. He is a part of the special Taskforce appointed by the Prime Minister's Office to re-configure Singapore's economy, and sits on various private and public boards and committees including the Monetary Authority of Singapore. ChinHwee co-wrote best-selling *Asian Financial Statement Analysis: Detecting Financial Irregularities*, which was published in English and Chinese, and does pro bono cases for regulators across the globe. He is a chartered financial analyst and chartered accountant, and fought the battle to have the words "for the benefit of society" included in the charter as president of CFA Singapore. Engaging in social work since his university days with his wife, he enjoys spending time with his three children.

Thomas Grandjean has worked in the commodities sector for the past 15 years. He graduated with a Master of Science in Economics from the University of Lausanne in Switzerland and is a CFA charter holder. He has lived in the Middle East, the United Kingdom, and Switzerland, and currently resides in Singapore.